MOVING THE NEEDLE

JOSH SUMMERSGILL

ISBN-13: 979-8-4880-7157-5

"Josh is one of the most genuine people I have ever met. He's a wealth of knowledge, yet he still constantly pushes to learn more and pass on his wisdom. He's meticulous and passionate about everyone under his wing, and has an amazing focus on progress and performance. Josh is the epitome of a coach. With the perfect balance of understanding, support and tough love."

Adam Travis – 2002 Commonwealth Weightlifting Championship Medalist

"The universal wisdom unearthed in the gym is so beautifully articulated for us all to enjoy for the benefit of our lives outside of it. This is so important and relatable".

Logan Gelbrich – Coach & Entrepreneur

"The best around at what he does. No frills, no nonsense. Josh is so much more than a coach. Although through working with Josh my ability, technique and performance numbers have improved dramatically, I have gained so much more mentally. These mental developments have carried over into my day to day life."

Mark Banner – Athlete, Client & Close Friend

"A lot of what Josh talks about in Moving The Needle are key things to why I believe I have personally been successful. Either way, you're going to really enjoy reading it."

Kari Pearce – 6x CrossFit Games Athlete & 4x Fittest Woman in America

"This book is great! I think it's not only for athletes, but also for people who have never set foot in the gym or who are brand new to training!"

Fraer Morrow – English, British & European Weightlifting Champion

CONTENTS

FOREWORD

I was introduced to the weights room when I was 14-years old, that was 20-years ago….(fuck!) I was introduced to Josh 4-years ago and I have to say that in all my 20-years of sets, reps and pursuits of physical and mental fitness I have never met anyone more professional, personable and approachable than the man who wrote this book!

I have known Josh in both personal and professional capacities and what I find most impressive about this guy is both his discipline and his devotion to improvement, not only for himself, but for all those around him.

He's the type of guy who will play a game of chess with you after having never played before, he will lose, go away, reflect, learn, practice and come back again and again and again until he learns how to beat you. Josh takes this approach to every challenge he faces in life, he'll try it, if he loses he'll develop a plan of attack, break it down, practice and try again and again and again until he cracks it. He's the first to admit when he was wrong and made a mistake and he's the first to take accountability and turn his failure into a lesson, because of this approach the man is mentally bullet proof! He is always willing to try new things and his comfort zone is more like a comfort continent because of his mentality and approach to life. This is what makes Josh an inspiring friend and great guy to have in your list of contacts!

What makes Josh an exceptional coach is nothing to do with the fact that the man is like a walking encyclopaedia of training, programming, weightlifting and nutritional knowledge! Nor is it anything to do with the fact that he lives the life that he promotes and sells to his clients. The thing that makes Josh an exceptional coach is that he cares, he truly cares about all the people who turn to him for answers and entrust him to help them reach their own goals. Josh is completely committed to every single one of his clients, he helps you realise very quickly that your goals are now his goals too and he walks with you on your road to self-improvement every step of the way. He celebrates your victories and he points out the lessons you can learn from your mistakes and he fully commits himself to helping you be all you can be.

'Moving the Needle' is a book for anyone and everyone. It is a collection of anecdotes and discoveries Josh has experienced, developed and discovered through years of mistakes, commitment and hard work that can be applied to all walks of life and living. The book won't do it for you and you won't unlock the meaning of life within its pages. What the book can do for you is give you a new perspective on challenges you may be facing both in the gym and out of it. It will motivate and inspire you to develop your own comfort zone and try new things and it will constantly remind you that perfection shouldn't be the mission, it's all about progression and moving the needle……oh NOW I get the title, clever!

- Craig Whittaker

MOVING THE NEEDLE

INTRODUCTION

On October 15th 1997, the ThrustSSC became the fastest car on the planet by breaking the World Land Speed record and hitting an astonishing 763mph. Not only that, but it also became the first car on record to ever break the sound barrier. The team behind creating the ThrustSSC worked tirelessly and were driven on by one specific goal, the goal of creating a car that could travel faster than any of its predecessors. It was simply a question of looking at that speedometer and asking themselves one thing above all else... "how do we move the needle?".

To power the ThrustSSC, the car was fitted with not one, but two Rolls Royce jet engines, which provided the equivalent of 110,000 bhp. To put this into perspective, that's more power than 140 Lamborghini Aventadors, or more than 1000 Ford Fiestas. The ThrustSSC was also fitted with specially designed active suspension to stop the nose from rising as it approached remarkable speeds. It's design even included a hidden rocket motor that was located in the nose of the car. In the event of the car hitting a bump in the road and lifting, the rocket would fire to apply a massive dump of downwards force to prevent this incredible machine going into orbit.

The team behind this record-breaking vehicle left no stone unturned. If there was any juice left to squeeze, they would squeeze it, and on that special day in 1997, all of their hard work and dedication had been worth it.

Throughout my career as a coach, I came to realise that what I was teaching people in the gym, had an incredible carry over into their day to day lives. Now I'm not talking about how a Deadlift can teach you to lift up a box of flat pack furniture, or how taking a bar from your shoulders to overhead can help you play with your children, it was the psychological lessons that were creating the biggest impact. It is these psychological discoveries and thought-provoking realisations that I want to share with *you*.

Through training, whether that be for a competitive sport or so that you can become fitter, stronger and live for longer, it's not just your physiology that adapts, more importantly, it's your mind. When you decide that just because something is challenging or uncomfortable, that doesn't mean that you stop or give up, that is when the real magic begins to happen. There are times in training when you would rather do anything else than complete your next set. It could be another 500m interval on the rower, it could be another set of supramaximal Clean pulls, it could even be when you're stuck up a mountain unable to walk properly. Regardless of what your task is, once you realise that you can physically get through it by being mentally resilient, there won't be much on planet earth that can stop you.

Through coaching, I learnt that as a coach you are not simply somebody who instructs a person through exercise. You develop a bond with that person and help them grow not only physically, but psychologically as well. I consider it an absolute privilege to call myself a coach, and that I have been able to coach so many unbelievable human beings since I started. To be able to truly have a positive impact on somebody's life is one of the best feelings in the world.

The reason I wrote this book is to share what I have learnt with as many people as possible. I want to share the lessons that I have seen first-hand have an amazing effect of peoples' lives. I wanted to create a book where as the reader you can not only enjoy the content, but I want to actively encourage you to scribble all over it. Make notes, underline elements that really resonate with you and use it as a reference manual. If like me you like to keep your books looking pristine, I have included a specific notes section in the back of the book for you to write in. Along with the notes section there is a reference list explaining any of the technical gym-based lingo.

You will find that throughout the book, there are a wide variety of chapters, varying from short easily digestible sections, to longer more in-depth stories. Although this book is not going to change your life overnight, I am a strong believer that the lessons, discoveries, and personal fuck ups throughout the pages to come can help you along your road to success, whether you are an athlete, casual gym goer, or somebody who has never stepped foot in a gym.

Through coaching, training, and often times learning things the hard way, the lessons learnt in this book are there to help you move forward with your performance, happiness and success. Whatever you aspire to achieve, it's time to start Moving The Needle!

CHAPTER ONE

PLAY THE LONG GAME

Instant gratification is lovely. Why work really hard for something when you can have the satisfaction of having it instantly? In today's society we find ourselves in a world that craves instant gratification. Whether you want to pin the blame on the pressure from our peers or social media, the fact is that nobody wants to play the long game.

Now I'd like to present you with a choice. Would you rather have one cookie now? Or 2 cookies later? Put another way, you can have something mediocre now, or you can have something great at a later date?

Everybody wants to be seen as being great at what they do. Whether that is their job, their hobbies, or a new skill that they have learnt. That's fine, that's just human nature. We strive for greatness and rightly so. But we don't only want greatness nowadays, we want it right now. Not tomorrow, not in a few years' time, right now.

Weightlifting & CrossFit are no different, especially amongst newer athletes. There is a famous soviet squat programme called "Smolov", which is designed to significantly increase the squat strength of the lifter. The problem with Smolov is that in only a matter of weeks, you can see crazy progress in your squat numbers, however because of the sheer volume and intensity of the programme, most none elite level athletes end up broken after the first cycle. Hips, knees, back or all 3. The programme takes its toll on the body and the majority of people end up further back than where they started. Regardless of this, newer lifters are still not put off and will try it anyway. 15kg added to your personal best in 6 weeks, who wouldn't want that right?

When I was younger my dad presented me with a fictitious scenario. He asked me "which would you prefer, I can give you one million pounds, or I can give you one penny and a chess board. The penny starts on the first square on the chess board, and then moves along one square at a time until it has been on every square. Every time the coin moves a square, the money doubles". Obviously, the go to answer would be the million pounds, or the 15kg PB Squat in 6 weeks. What I was too young and naive to realise was what the value of that penny would be on the final square. There are 64 squares on a chess board, by the time you reach square number 30 you will already be past the one million pounds mark. Now let's do some more maths. If you could train injury free for 5 years, and add 1kg every month to a lift, that is a whopping 60kg over the space of 5 years. If the magic Tin Slingin' genie came and offered me a 60kg increase on my Snatch in 5 years, it's safe to say I'd bite his hand off!

The number one issue with instant gratification is that you never get a true sensation of accomplishment. Imagine if you have never played the piano, but you go round to your friend's house and they have one in their back room. You jump on, decide to give it a bash, and all of sudden you're playing Beethoven's Moonlight Sonata. Granted this would be pretty cool for a moment, but there would be no sense of achievement. The same is true for when somebody first starts CrossFit and Handstand Walking comes up. For the lucky few that can do it with minimal practice, it becomes just another trivial movement, but for the person who has tried, failed, practiced for 18 months and then finally gets their first 12 feet, now that is magical moment!

CHAPTER TWO

BECOME THE TRAIT THAT YOU WISH TO POSSESS

"I wish I had as much discipline as X", "I wish I had the confidence that Y has", "if only I was as driven as Z". There are many traits that different individuals wished that they possessed. These can be traits that friends or family have, or maybe someone inspirational who they know. But rather than aspiring to simply have a trait, for example "I wish I had more dedication", aspire to make that trait a part of who you are. Don't *wish* to have more dedication, strive to "*be* dedicated".

Having powerful traits as part of your identity can be an incredibly potent set of tools to help you tackle anything that life may throw at you. You're feeling tired and flat, but you have 2 more sets of 10 to complete whilst training. You never abandon the sets because YOU ARE somebody that gets the work done, or YOU ARE somebody that doesn't stop when things get tough.

Rather than getting a takeaway on a Wednesday night because you've had a tough day, you cook the chicken that you have in the fridge because YOU ARE somebody that sticks to the plan. You started on your quest to lose weight 4 weeks ago and you're not going to fail now just because you've not had a great day.

However, even the most dedicated of people have stumbles and face challenges. If you fail at something, you ARE NOT somebody who always fails. If you miss a gym session because your car breaks down, you ARE NOT somebody that misses training. Absorb the positive traits, make them part of who you are, but disregard the negatives, these are simply potholes in your road to success!

Next time you find yourself wishing that you had a trait, take a moment to stop and think. If you can begin to rewire your thought process so that you can start to believe that you can make your desired trait part of who you are, with repetition and practice, this way of thinking will start to build up momentum and before you realise it you will be well on your way to moving the needle.

CHAPTER THREE

YOU CAN SLOW DOWN BUT YOU CAN'T STOP

Training has its ups and downs, as does day to day life. It has some very high highs, and some equally low lows. If you stop and throw the towel in, that's it, game over. But, if you keep on chipping away, even at a snail's pace, session by session, you'll end up one hell of a lot closer to where you want to be than if you had stopped.

Making progress at anything can be looked at as a collection of sessions built up over an extended period of time. You become better at putting a golf ball by practicing putting thousands of times. Singers perfect their voice by repeatedly singing and rehearsing, and people who are great entrepreneurs have failed more times than they have succeeded. The one thing they all have in common is that they never stopped. Regardless of how slow the progress.

This lesson is something that I carried with me when I tried to run my first marathon. Bear in mind that I'm predominantly a power athlete, and up until this point the furthest I had run without stopping was around 5 miles. That being said, waking up one morning and randomly deciding to run 26.2 miles around the perimeter of Warrington where I live sounded like a great idea. With minimal endurance training, all I took with me was some gels and water, my hubris and the internal reminder that "I can slow down, but I can't stop".

After eating a light breakfast and drinking a black coffee, I did what you could almost class as a warmup, and then got ready to roll. I walked out of the front door, put the key in my zip pocket and took a deep breath. With my headphones on and my confidence high, I set off on my 26 mile bad idea.

As with any endurance event, or anything that takes more than 10 minutes, the beginning is always a challenge because you haven't found your rhythm yet. Your body hasn't had time to settle in and everything feels a little awkward and stiff. For the first half a mile, that's exactly how I felt. The gears hadn't yet been greased and I hadn't found my stride. But once I hit the mile 1 marker, everything began to smoothen out. It was at this point that David Goggins chirped up in my headphones with the phrase "you don't stop when it hurts, you stop when you're done!". "FUCK YEH, LET'S GO" was my first reaction, until I quickly remembered that I had another 25 miles left to run and sprinting would not be conducive to my survival. So, I held back my inner Usain Bolt and kept with my pace.

The next 5 miles went so well that I kept having moments of thinking "oh wow how have I got here?". I was comfortably running whilst zoning in and out of an audio book. I remember thinking to myself how great my running felt, I was effortlessly gliding over the pavement one foot after another. The same thing carried on for the next 5 miles. At mile 10, I was genuinely considering hitting the finish line and doing a second lap. "If I'm going to do 26.2 miles and they all feel as great as this first 10, then hell to it let's do 50!". Naive moron.

My temporary state of running euphoria continued for the next 2 miles. I decided that as I'd brought 3 gels, that now would be a good time to top up my carb levels. I felt myself dropping off slightly, so it was more a case of a pre-emptive strike before I crashed completely. I consumed my gel whilst trying to decide if it's classed as eating or drinking, and motored on.

Even if you're having the best dream in the world, you still have to wake up, and my alarm clock began to sing load and clear just before mile 13. My left knee that has given me grief in the past decided that it wanted to make an appearance. I was able to ignore if at first, but it wasn't long before every step was causing a shooting pain through the inside of my knee. "You're fine, it's just discomfort, and discomfort equals adaptation". The internal dialogue in my head was reassuring, but sadly incorrect. Discomfort had now turned into pain.

As I approached the halfway mark, the route that I was following brought me out on a small road near the gym where I train. Once you come to the end of the path and move onto the road, you're presented with a nasty incline up a bridge over a river. I've ran over this bridge countless times in the past when doing workouts at the gym, but this time I could have sworn that somebody had made it steeper. As I struggled up the bridge, my hip flexors and adductors began to violently cramp and spasm. I tried to lift my knees to get up the hill, but my body was now rebelling even further. My carbs had dropped, my salt levels had deteriorated, and I had officially bonked.

It had taken me just under 2 hours to complete the first half of a marathon, and at that point I knew that the second half would not be the same story. With my body in bits, my stubbly jog slowed down to a walk and I was absolutely furious with myself. Every ounce of me did not want to go from a run to a walk, but even though I felt disappointed, I reminded myself of the phrase that I set off with, "you can slow down, but you can't stop!".

At this point, as I was walking, I had to come up with a new plan of attack. I had 12 miles left to go, no supplies and only 250ml of water left of the original 750ml that I brought with me. My initial plan was to run for a minute, and then walk for a minute. In my head this seemed perfectly feasible and would be considerably quicker than walking to the finish line. But as soon as I tried to break into anything faster than a walk, my hip flexors and adductors wouldn't have it. So, I was now stuck with walking.

Another 2 arduous miles completed, and at mile 16 I was presented with a choice. At this point on the route lay a roundabout. Exit 1 would take me along the route I had mapped out, and exit 2 would take me almost directly to my house. I wanted nothing more than to tell Morpheus to stick it, take the blue pill and take exit 2 and make a beeline for home, but what would be the point. I was already in pain, I had already covered 16 miles, if I was to quit now I'd still be in pain, and I'd then have to contend with the mental pain of failure as well. I'd like to say I had a moment of inspiration, the clouds parted and a beam of light shone down on me as I marched on with purpose, but that's not what happened. I did take exit 1 and carried on, but I resembled an angry teenager who had just been asked to tidy their room. With my strop in tow, I carried on.

The 4 miles that followed were practically a stumble through the desert. The route that I had followed had no particular landmarks or interesting paths, it was a long winding country road that seemed to never end. I was completely out of water at this point, and was also walking down a road that I had actually never been down before. I began to fantasise about cold pints of juice or glass of Coke poured over ice. This then caused another dilemma. If I was to find a shop on route, would I go in to get a drink? Because technically, this would mean stopping.

As the miles slowly ticked down and the sunburn on my face got progressively redder, no shop appeared. With 2 miles to go I had come to the conclusion that pulling out my phone and ringing for a lift was definitely out of the question. I was going to make it across the finish line and it was just a case of how long it would actually take me.

When I initially planned out the 26.2 mile circuit, I had done so in such a way that the finish line was around 400m from my house. The run was to finish just past the Dominos warehouse, and then the theory was that after all that running, I could have a nice leisurely cool down walk back to my front door. Everything's great in theory right. So, when I came over the brow of a hill and I could see the warehouse in the distance it felt like a mirage, I was nearly home!

Knowing that I was less than a mile away from completing my first marathon, I decided to try to run as a final push to get to the finish, but once again my legs did not agree with my mind. It didn't matter at this point, my limp became a strut as I proudly turned the corner onto the final stretch of road. As I did so, for the first time since the start of the "run" I pulled out my phone to see the damage. I pulled up Strava to see the figures. To my horror, I had only covered a distance of 25.2 miles. The Dominos warehouse was literally in touching distance, and it was at the point I realised that I'd fucked up!

Just when I thought it was over, I had another mile left to go. I looked down at my watch, 5 hours and 50 minutes. This was probably the worst thing that I could have done because now, I had convinced myself that even though I hadn't been able to run for the last 4 hours, by some kind of divine intervention I would be able to get the last mile done in under 10 minutes and finish in under 6 hours. For a final time, I threw myself forward in an attempt to run. I managed less than 10 steps before I had to return to my stumble once again.

After a grand total of 6 hours and 12 minutes I crossed the finish line, but it wasn't without one final slap in the face. When I finally reached my front door, Strava confirmed that I had another 200m left to go. I laughed as I passed the front of my house to do a lap of honour round the estate, my final punishment from the gods of fitness for being an idiot.

Dehydrated, sunburnt and barely able stand, but it was totally worth it. I opened my front door, sank 2 pints of the most amazing blackcurrant juice I had ever tasted, and sat on the floor. I had slowed down, but I hadn't stopped.

The man that walks one mile a day for a year, covers more ground than the man that runs 13 marathons. Always keeping pushing on!

CHAPTER FOUR

THE PATH ALREADY WALKED IS EASIER TO FOLLOW

At some point we've all been in a position where we're trying to get to a destination, and we've got lost. Your sat nav starts telling you to go down roads that no longer exist, you start giving your partner grief for being a hopeless co-pilot, and your kids are kicking off in the back because that's what kids do. In contrast to this we've also all been to places that we have visited many times before, and I think we can all agree that these places are easier to get to.

The same theory can be applied to training. If we say that your all time Deadlift 1 rep max is 100kg, but that was 5 years ago and you haven't really trained much since then. You begin training again and within a few weeks, you hit a 70kg Deadlift as a new baseline. The question is, are you going to find it easier to get back to 100kg, than if you had never been there previously? Absolutely. Because you have already hit a 100kg Deadlift in the past, you have already leaped over several hurdles that could potentially be in your way if it was unknown territory.

One of the main limiting factors that people face with performance, both inside and outside of training, is the mental limitations that they put on themselves. Self-doubt and a lack of believe can limit you more than most other factors. If you have already Deadlifted 100kg, you know that it is possible, you have at some point done this, and therefore you believe that it can be done again.

Now there are other elements that have to be considered. Just because you Snatched 150kg at the Olympics when you were 21, that does not mean that you can do it again when you're 65. This concept is all within reason and isn't necessarily true for elite level performance.

The main thing to be aware of is that your body remembers. Once upon a time your body adapted to Deadlifting 100kg, both physiologically and psychologically, and those adaptions don't just disappear. They may go dormant but they certainly don't just vanish.

CHAPTER FIVE

STRESS IS STRESS

The human mind can only spin so many plates at any one time, as a result, it can also only deal with certain amount of stress in one go. We all deal with multiple stressors on a day-to-day basis and cope perfectly well. Family, Relationship, Work, Financial, Training, these are all different types of stress that can take up valuable cognitive space. Some days nothing gets to us, and other days it can feel like somebody is just piling it on top of us. The dark clouds roll in and it becomes "one of those days".

For those of you who go to the gym for recreational purposes, and to work towards general health and fitness, a gym session can be the perfect remedy for a stressful day. You can rock up, hit a session and release some endorphins. However, for those of us who train for a sport or competition, the opposite can be true. Rather than the gym being time to decompress, it can actually become another stressor. If you're worrying about paying bills, or problems at work, you're going to find it very tough to hit something technical like a max effort Clean & Jerk.

Whilst there is not a great deal that can be done to remove the issue all together, what we can do is learn to acknowledge the fact that stress is stress. If we're worrying about other aspects of our life, they are going to have an impact on something like our training. It's important to note that every single one of us needs to take the time out to decompress. If you don't train competitively, then the gym can be perfect "you time". If you do train for competition though, a daily walk or quiet morning meditation would be more adequate.

CHAPTER SIX

PLAY SILLY GAMES, WIN SILLY PRIZES

As human beings, we love to learn things the hard way. Most of the time even though we know something is a bad idea because somebody has told us, we try it anyway just in case they're wrong. When I was in my late teens, I went to look at a new car. It was a bright yellow 2 litre turbo hot hatch that my friends later christened "The Yellow Peril". Being young and foolish I thought this car was amazing, but my dad thought otherwise. He told me that buying this car was a terrible idea, it would fall to bits because that particular make was renowned for doing so, and I'd lose a fortune on it. Needless to say, I ignored his advice bought the Peril, and within 6 months the aircon unit had broken, both the electric windows had stopped working, and the boot lid had fell off. Egg on face.

One of the athletes that I coach came up to me once and asked if she could do another workout on that particular day. Now so far, she had already completed a 2 hour Weightlifting session in the morning, then 2 CrossFit workouts after that. About an hour or so after the second CrossFit workout she asked me if she could do another workout. Obviously, I told her that this was a terrible idea, and she doesn't need any more training volume for that day. However, she insisted that she really wanted to do this next workout, at which point I agreed and told her to crack on

.

The next day, this particular athlete rocked up to do her session and if I was to say she was useless, that would be an understatement. After barely getting through a half-hearted warm up, we had to drop her workload dramatically so that she could get through her session. After finally completing the session, she came up to me and muttered "I really shouldn't have done that extra workout". Being the humble person that I am simply gave her a smile that basically said “Oh really? That’s weird” and agreed.

To this day Nat still reminds me of how this is one of the most important lessons she has ever learnt. If you go off programme and do 4 times your normal training volume, you're going to have the fatigue that comes with it. Likewise, if you don't listen to your dad's advice and buy a stupid car, you're going to spend a fortune fixing it.

Before you move onto the next chapter, take a moment to stop and think about a time when you have made a mistake and won your own silly prize. Is there a lesson that can be learnt from it, is there something that can be taken from it to help you in the future? It's not a crime to make mistakes, it's a crime not to learn from them.

CHAPTER SEVEN

TAKE THE FIRST STEP

For some strange reason, the vast majority of us expect to be able to do something new either straight away, or not at all. You'll either attempt to try a new skill and be able to do it, or you won't be able to do it and think "well I'm not very good at that". The thing is, nobody can do anything perfectly the first time they try, some maybe better than others, but nobody throws a javelin a world record distance on their first attempt.

Now let's look at the Snatch. The Snatch is one of the most difficult sporting movements the human body can perform. The athlete takes the bar from the ground and catches it over their head in a deep squat, before standing up to complete the movement. At the top level this bar can be more than double the lifter's bodyweight. So it's safe to say this movement is pretty difficult. Are you going to nail Snatching on your first session? Absolutely not. You're going to make a right car crash of it, and you know what, that's absolutely fine.

The same can be said when you start a new job, wallpaper the house for the first time, or you become the designated chef at home. At first your job will be tough, and you'll mess up more than you get right, the first lot of wallpaper will look textured because there will be that many creases in it, and the first few meals you cook will only be fit for the dog. But again, that's absolutely fine.

What you've done here is take the first step. You've accepted that when you start something new, you're probably going to suck at it to begin with. If you can apply this simple realisation to anything that you want to learn, you'll have one less massive hurdle to clear. Don't put off starting something new because you don't want to be seen to be terrible at it.

CHAPTER EIGHT

YOU RESPOND TO YOUR ENVIRONMENT

If it's cold your body shivers, if it's hot your body sweats, if the room is positive, you will feel more positive, and if the atmosphere in the room is dull and negative you will feel duller and more negative.

If you're training goals are to be fitter, stronger and live healthier, but to have fun in the process, then you want to plunge yourself into a training environment whereby you're going to enjoy yourself. Whether that be a community-based gym, or a class with your friends, if your training environment is a pleasant place to be, then you're going to respond to that in a positive way.

On the flip side, if you're training for competition, then it's going to be beneficial for you to train in an environment full of people like yourself who will push you. If you train in an environment where everybody wants to compete, but pushes each other up collectively, then you're going to push yourself further than if you were the only competitor.

Before I dove headfirst out of the 9am to 5pm plane many years back, I used to work in an office. Having spent 8 years in the job I moved around quite a bit between offices. Now some of them were brilliant, I worked with and met some amazing people, some of whom I'm still close friends with today. However, there were also some that were the total opposite.

There was one office in particular where I was based for around 9 months, and you have never seen a sadder looking building. The office itself had been around for years and in parts was not too dissimilar to a prison. During this time, I responded to the negativity within the building and began to hate every day that I was there. There was nobody there at the time who was either of similar age or who I had similar interests with, which only added to the situation. This particular spell was one of the catalysts that helped me jump ship and pursue what I actually love doing.

If you ever find yourself in an environment that you don't like, you have one of two choices. You can either move away from it, or you can influence change and make it a more positive place. You can't always control your environment, but you can always choose it. Are you happy where you are? If the answer is "Yes", that's brilliant, crack on. If the answer is "No", then it's time to step to it and do something about it.

CHAPTER NINE

TYPE 'A' TENDENCIES

As a species we are all very similar, but for all the similarities we share, we also have just as many differences. One difference in particular is that of our personality. What we are like as individuals, our views and our behaviours.

On the whole, the vast majority of people fall into 1 of 2 categories, Type 'A' or Type 'B'. Type As tend to be high achievers, and always push themselves to be the top 1% of whatever they do. Type 'A's are also extremely competitive, whether with others or themselves, and once they make a plan, they stick to it and see it through to the end.

Type 'B's on the other hand, are essentially the total opposite. They're not particularly competitive and are not too concerned with being the best of the best. Type 'B's are also a lot more "go with the flow", relaxed, and tend just roll with an idea and see what happens. Is one wrong and one right? Absolutely not. They're as different as red and blue, but neither one is correct. However, regardless of which category you fall into, there are particular type 'A' traits that can be extremely powerful.

Competition is a good thing. And in a world of participation medals and "everyone is a winner", the essence of not only competing, but the desire to push oneself to beat somebody is starting to dwindle. If the lion doesn't catch the wildebeest, the pride goes hungry. If that lion doesn't win, the rest don't eat. If you have the desire to win, you can apply that to absolutely anything that you go after in day-to-day life.

Winning doesn't have to mean beating somebody else. Winning can mean overcoming something challenging, either physically or mentally. You're in the gym, feeling flat and you have one more set left. Are you going to give in and let it beat you? You go through a tough relationship break up and 12 months later you're still moping around feeling sorry for yourself. Are you going to let this beat you and keep you in the dumps for ever?

Whichever personality category you fall under, if any, take the best bits from both. If you can flip the switch and be as chilled out as a type 'B', but then when it's game time you can be as competitive as a type 'A', you're going to have a greater chance of conquering your goals.

CHAPTER TEN

STOP WINGING IT

Freestyling, going with the flow and making it up as you go along is great, but it will only get you so far. It is a great skill to possess as you don't hold back from starting something without having a bulletproof plan. However, if you want to truly get the most out of something, you need to make a plan.

When my old business partner and I first started out, something that we were particularly good at was winging it. Even though we had plans and strategies in place for some things, most aspects of what we were doing were learnt on the fly and we improvised as we developed and grew. Again, whilst this was great to start with, it was only once we started to implement strategies, targets and procedures did we start to see any real progress.

Without an effective plan of action, you're not going to get the results you want as optimally as possible. The benefit of having an actionable plan is that you can effectively point all your efforts towards the designated target, without wasting time.

The same can be said for training. If you're looking to get better or to compete in weightlifting, you need to follow a weightlifting programme. Rather than just turning up to the gym and doing a bit of this and a bit of that, if you're looking to make significant improvements you need to follow a progressive structure. If you're looking to complete a 100 mile ultra-run through the Swiss Alps, and you don't follow a programme, you're going to fail. Just like if you wake up and randomly decide that you're going to run a marathon with zero preparation… and as we've learnt from chapter 3, we all know how that went. What can I say, we're only human.

Whenever you have a task to complete, potentially something like a 10,000 word dissertation for your degree, if you make a plan to write 'x' number of words a day, or 'y' number of pages a week, you're going to get through the workload more efficiently and effectively.

When I set out to write this book, I set myself a target to write at least one chapter every day. Instead of motoring through a chunk of work on the days that I felt motivated, and then do nothing for weeks, I completed a couple of pages a day. As a result, this meant that I was able to finish the book by the target date that I had set myself.

Next time you're setting out to complete a task, come up with a battle plan before diving in head first. It doesn't need to be perfect, and it sure as hell doesn't need to be complex, keep it simple and effective and see how efficient and optimal you can become.

CHAPTER ELEVEN

LOVE WHAT YOU DO

Everybody has their own individual "why" when it comes to something like training. Some people start exercising to lose weight, some people start swimming because they enjoy doing something with friends, and some people start training because they want to compete and see how far they can progress. All of these drivers are perfectly valid and will be useful when it comes to pushing through those challenging days. However, what about if you just love what you do? You do something for the sheer love of it?

When I was in primary school, I was introduced to Judo. This was the first martial art that I had ever tried, and I stuck at it for just over 12 months. Since then, I have tried numerous different disciplines including Muay Thai, Wing Chun, Krav Maga, and finally the one that I truly enjoyed, Kickboxing.

I started kickboxing 8 years ago. I originally started because a close friend of mine had recently joined and had asked me to come down and try it out. It was brilliant. The class was great, the instructor was inspiring and the other students were very welcoming. As a result, I stayed with the club for 4 years, progressing all the way up to brown 3, the final belt before black belt. Since the first grading, I became obsessed with achieving a black belt. I turned up to every session thinking about how proud I would feel to eventually wear that belt.

Unfortunately, my instructor and myself had to part ways just months before I was due to take my black belt grading. As a result, I went on the hunt for other local kickboxing clubs that I could potentially join where I could finish my black belt training.

After speaking to several clubs, I was met with the same answer every time. I would be more than welcome to join, but because of the federation that my previous gradings were under, I would have to start from the very beginning... white belt. At the time, this realisation crippled me. The thought of 4 years "wasted" because I would have to start again from day 1 was too much, so I stopped kickboxing all together.

2 years had passed and I still hadn't thought about taking it back up. I had a dabble with Taekwondo for a bit during the interim, but it wasn't really my thing. It was only when I received a text message from a couple that I used to help coach at my first kickboxing club, that I began to think about it once more.

The couple had found a new club, and they absolutely loved it. They couldn't speak more highly of the instructor and of the students. After toying with the idea, I decided to go down and try out the class, after all, I had nothing to lose.

Just as I did 8 years previous, I absolutely loved my first class. I explained my situation to the instructor and as expected, I was once again told that I would have to start from white belt. But this time it was different. I was no longer obsessed with achieving a black belt, I just simply loved kickboxing and wanted to do it for the sheer enjoyment. My '*why*' had totally changed.

To the present day, I am still with my new club. I love every session and enjoy every minute. Although I find myself only 2 belts away from black belt once again, it is not that which makes me carry on coming. I do it because I love it, and the best part is that the belt will come along with it anyway.

Do whatever you do for the love of it.

CHAPTER TWELVE

PUT YOUR PHONE AWAY

I think we can all collectively admit to being guilty of this one. You finish your set, re-rack the bar or dumbbells and whip out your phone. Then you begin to mindlessly scroll through Nike.com or Instagram, until minutes later you realise "oh shit, I'm actually in the gym and I need to complete another set". So you complete your next set and then the cycle starts all over again.

Why is this problematic? Surely whilst you're resting this can't be that much of an issue? It's not like you're performing hill sprints during your rest period. The issue is that you are not present. Training of any kind is not just some mindless monotonous task that you just "do", or at least it shouldn't be if done properly. If you have just completed a heavy set of Back Squats, and you have 3 minutes to rest, use those 3 minutes to actually rest. Sit down and allow your whole body to recover, including your mind. Whilst you're recovering, you can also now stay focused on the job at hand, which is squeezing every ounce out of your next set.

Here's a scenario for you. You're building to a max Snatch, it's 1 rep max time and it's game on. You hit a near maximal lift, it feels great, so now it's time to go for a new personal best. You load the bar, and then take a seat. Rather than sitting there and visualising hitting the perfect lift, you pull out your phone. You have received a message off the delivery company saying that your parcel has not been delivered and has been returned to the depot. Now rather than thinking about hitting a big lift, you're sat there fuming because you have to wait another 48 hours for your new trainers. You slam your phone down, walk up to the bar and make an absolute mess of the lift. You miss, it comes crashing down, and all because you checked your phone.

Your phone can be great, but more importantly it can imprison you. The next time you're in public, maybe in a coffee shop or having a meal, have a look around. If there are any couples about, watch what happens when one of them needs to get up to use the toilet. If the person staying by the table isn't already on it, watch them immediately pull their phone out. Once again this is something that we have all been guilty of, so let's work to change it. Next time you find yourself sat on your own, keep your phone in your pocket and allow yourself to think freely. You never know what creative and innovative ideas may come to you.

CHAPTER THIRTEEN

IT'S NOT MY FAULT

Nobody enjoys admitting that they were wrong or that something was their fault. It's much easier to shift the blame onto somebody or something else than it is to accept that it is down to you. Just like standing on a crosstrainer for 20 minutes is easier than doing a session of strength work and high intensity conditioning, but we all know which one is going to offer the greater reward in the long run.

But what if we were to change our perspective and start taking full responsibility for our actions. If your training isn't going well, rather than lashing out and blaming the training programme, could it be something that you're not doing yourself? Are you sleeping 4 hours a night, eating takeaways for lunch and stressing about your home life? Even the best programme in the world isn't going to help you out there.

You've got an important exam to sit, you're confident, feeling good and you head into the examination room. You come out 2 hours later in an emotional cocktail of rage, anger and frustration. "That test was BS! Why would they word it like this, why would they want to know that?". Is the test at fault? Maybe it's the people who wrote the test, it must be their fault? The only person whose fault it isn't is your own. Could you have maybe studied more effectively? Could you have revised more? Could you have been more prepared?

Once you make the leap and start taking full ownership of everything you do, not only do you empower yourself, but also other people will respect you. If you're in a position of trust or influence, whether that's a coach, mentor, parent or friend, you have the ability to show others that it's perfectly acceptable to mess up, because trust me we all do. If you can own it, you can learn from it.

CHAPTER FOURTEEN

YOU EITHER WIN OR LEARN

Whether during competition in sport, job interviews or taking an exam, you win some and you lose some. Even the best of the best have suffered losses at some point in their career. The difference between the best and the rest, is that when the best in the business get beat, it's not a loss, it's a lesson. Yes, they didn't win, but what can they learn so that next time they can come back and take the victory.

During preparation for the recent online national Weightlifting Championships, my build up to the competition was going great. Outside of training, everything from my nutrition, my rehab, my mindset and my recovery was on point. Training itself was also going well, I was physically stronger than I had ever been. On the cycle prior to the competition taper I'd hit all time personal best Back Squats and Deadlifts, so I felt confident carrying that strength over into the competition lifts, the Snatch and the Clean & Jerk.

A week out and everything was still on point. Ice baths had become part of my daily routine, as did regular visualisation work. I'd picture myself hitting specific numbers on the day. I'd visualise everything from the crowd, my barbell approach, even the music in the background. My body weight was almost bang on and I was ready for action.

The night before, I readied myself for the big day. I relaxed, prepared my kit, and got an early night. When D Day arrived, I woke up filled with excitement and couldn't wait to touch the barbell. First port of call, jump on the scales. Result, I'd hit weight and even had some wiggle room. This meant that I was able to grab a small bite to eat and an espresso. After a cold shower and a bit of food, it was time to get ready. I pulled on my singlet, put on my shorts and t-shirt and got ready to head to the gym.

We arrived at the gym 10 minutes before I was due for my official weigh in. After unloading the car, I paced up and down the gym waiting for the clock to hit 10am. As soon as "10:00" flashed up, I stripped down to my singlet to get my competition weight. It was great news once again. I was 0.2 of a kg under the weight limit. Because of the new rules in Weightlifting, it now favours you to be heavy in your category, and I couldn't have really planned it much better. Once I had weighed in, a 3 hour timer began to countdown. This was my window to complete my lifts.

First things first, as soon as I stepped off the scales it was time to eat like a horse. I threw down some food, replaced all my fluids and now it was time to get after it. I gave myself 45 minutes to digest and then I gradually began my warmup. This was the same warm up that I do every time I train. Competition day is no time to change things that don't need to be changed. As I was warming up, everything was moving well, I didn't really have any aches or pains, and my confidence was growing. I headed over to the barbell and began to build up.

Coming into the competition, I wanted to hit a 120kg Snatch and a 145kg Clean & Jerk. Now these are no record-breaking numbers, but for me they were big. I'd hit 120kg multiple times in training, but I'd never hit it in competition. As for the 145kg Clean & Jerk, I had Cleaned a 160kg in training a few weeks before, but I had recently switched my Jerk technique and had only ever hit a 141kg with this particular style. I knew I was capable of hitting what I set out to hit, all I had to do was execute.

It was now time to Snatch. I began to build up, hitting rep after rep of sharp technique. I remember hitting a particular 80kg and it felt like 40kg, it was going to be a good day. Things started to get serious once I had hit 106kg. The bar was now loaded at 111kg, and it was getting up there to the lifts that mattered. I approached the bar in the same manner that I had done so far for every lift previously. I hit my set up, took a deep breath and began to lift. Miss!

As soon as the bar separated from the floor, I remember thinking to myself in that split second "oh my god what is on this bar". It felt as though somebody had sneakily slid on an extra 10kg on each side. As a result, I made a mess of the lift and missed the bar out in front. Everybody misses lifts, and I put it to the back of my mind, shook it off, and minutes later went again. Missed again!

This time, self-doubt was no longer creeping in, it was coming in hot. And self-doubt wasn't the only problem I was trying to ignore. Frustration was also beginning to show its face. This was a weight that on a previous training phase I'd hit for a comfortable triple, so why on earth was I missing it now. Not only had I now convinced myself that 120kg was impossible, I was no longer confident that I could hit 111kg. On attempt number 3 I sealed my fate... miss.

I walked out of the gym to gather my thoughts and make sense of what had just happened. I was furious with myself. As far as I was concerned, I'd fell 14kg short of what I knew I could hit. Now as a coach, I know how to deal with athletes when they have a wobble, but when it's happening to you it's tough as hell to listen to your own advice. The Snatch part of the competition was what it was, and now I had to stop my head from rolling down the road, put it back on my shoulders, and go big on the Clean & Jerk.

Unlike the build-up on my Snatch, the build-up to my Clean & Jerk was lacklustre to say the least. I started missing warm up weights on the Jerk, and with my new technique, it was becoming even more frustrating. Warming up, I missed 125kg 3 times. It was then that I thought "fuck this" and resorted back to my old style of Jerking. Amazingly, I managed to pull through and hit every lift from there on in. My final lift was a decent 142kg, which all things considered I was pretty happy about. But deep down, I was raging with myself.

What a shit show. I Snatched just over 85% of my all-time best, and Clean & Jerked just over 90%. Even with everyone who had come to support me telling me that I did my best, I was fuming with myself and felt like a failure. I sulked and felt sorry for myself for a good 48 hours after the event.

It was only once the clouds had cleared that I was able to see the light. My emotions had calmed, and I was able to see my performance for what it was. Had I done everything I could building up to the comp? Absolutely. Did I give my 100 percent best effort on the day? Damn right I did. Is there anything I could have done differently? Only once the dust had settled and I'd spoken to my coach did the answer become clear.

During the previous cycle before the comp prep phase, I had responded extremely well to the design of the cycle. However, during the comp prep phase, the opposite was true. I hadn't peaked how I should have done and my lifts at the comp confirmed this. Now was this my coach's fault? Absolutely not. Neither me nor my coach were to know that this particular prep cycle wouldn't work for me, but guess what, now we do.

I didn't lose at the online national championships, what I actually did was learn. I learnt a valuable lesson about how I should and more importantly should not taper for competition… but the story doesn't end there.

4 months after my internal disaster, I once again stepped onto the platform to lift. This time it wasn't a virtual competition, this time it was The British Open, and it was in front of 150+ spectators, officials, and cameras pointed in my face. With nowhere to hide and the pressure on, the question was, would the past come back to haunt me, or had I truly slayed that demon? Had I learnt from my mistakes? Fucking right I had! After hitting my 110kg opener, I then went onto hit what is possibly the best 115kg Snatch of my life, which was also a competition PB. I finished the day with a new personal best competition total, but more importantly and above all, I had won internally.

The feeling of that personal victory was magnified incredibly and was so much sweeter because of my previous failure. If I had never failed, I would never feel as proud as I do now.

If you weren't successful during a job interview, ask yourself or the interviewers why and learn from it. Did your friend beat you at chess? If so how and why? You can always use these lessons to help you become better and more successful.

CHAPTER FIFTEEN

SCHEDULE IN YOUR TRAINING

How many times have you heard the phrase "I didn't get round to going to the gym today"? You may have even said it yourself. To be fair, in the fast pace busy busy era that we find ourselves in, it's perfectly understandable how you can struggle to find time in the day to do everything that you'd like to do. However, there is a solution.

If you say to yourself, "Right I'm going to get up, complete task X, Y & Z, then I'll try and get to the gym before I go for coffee with my friend", the chances are that you will not go to the gym. You'll more than likely run out of time before you have to go for coffee and your training session will disappear. On the other hand, you are more than likely going to meet up with your friend simply because you have put it in your diary. You have agreed a time and a place, and your friend is going to be there waiting.

Now let's replan that day, scheduling in your priorities. You're meeting your friend at 2, so you schedule your gym time for midday, as opposed to "if I get chance". You then work backwards and allocate a specific amount of time to complete tasks X, Y & Z. You may realise that you have to get up 30 minutes earlier to fit everything in, but it's definitely worth it. No more missed training sessions.

If something is really important to you, make sure you schedule it in. Your free time will unknowingly to you become consumed with filler and unimportant tasks. Whether it is seeing your family, training or catching up with your friends, schedule it in!

CHAPTER SIXTEEN

COMFORT IS KILLING YOUR PROGRESS

Once you become comfortable doing something, the chances are that you are no longer improving. You have reached a point whereby the task at hand is comfortable and easy to perform, and therefore you are no longer forcing an adaptation. To become better, you must challenge yourself, and that usually involves being uncomfortable.

A couple of years ago, a friend of mine and I decided that we were sick of being terrible at swimming, so we sought out a swim coach and we began weekly swim sessions. To put it into perspective, I wouldn't drown in the bath, but one 25m length of a pool would kill me, which for somebody who considers themselves as relatively fit, was pretty frustrating.

One session in particular, our coach told us that we were to complete some hypoxic lengths. This basically meant swimming lengths without breathing, and needless to say, it was pretty god damn uncomfortable. There was nothing leisurely about almost drowning, but after a few weeks, surprise surprise we both started to improve.

Many years back I had a new client come down to the gym to try a 1-2-1 session. Like anybody joining a gym they wanted to get fitter, stronger and healthier and were excited to start training. They had never done any Weightlifting before, so it was a completely new experience. However, halfway through the session we had to stop because "the bar was too rough and was hurting their hands". Now this wasn't an Eleiko Competition bar (a barbell that tears your hands to pieces), this was a training bar with next to no knurling on it.

We moved on from the barbell and tried a variety of different movements, all of which were also uncomfortable in some way shape or form. After the session had finished, I thanked them for coming down and concluded that I was not the right coach for this person, and we went our separate ways.

To truly get better and develop we need to remove ourselves from the comfort zone. Ditch the bar pads and the ergonomically developed pulley grips that feel lovely in your hands. If you want to compete at something, go for a competition that is going to challenge you. I'd rather finish last at the world championships than first in local in-house comp.

David Goggins talks about when a sword is forged, it is plunged into the fire and has the shit beaten out of it. Become the sword, not a wet flannel.

CHAPTER SEVENTEEN

CELEBRATE THE SMALL VICTORIES

If you work really hard for something it deserves to be acknowledged. Not necessarily by others, but certainly by yourself. Small and seemingly unimportant little wins add up to winning the war. If these little wins are to go unnoticed, then they just become part of a routine.

Let's say you're training and you're working through your session. Last week you managed 8 reps at a particular weight, but this week you managed to squeeze out a 9th, that right there is a win! You get to Sunday night, and you realise that you have stretched and done your mobility work for 7 days on the bounce, that's another small victory! Recently you decided that you wanted to get leaner and lose some body weight, this week you lost half a kilogram... that's a win!

Now let's flip it. Every night before you go to bed you prep your food for work the following day. You do this because not only is it healthier than going to the bakery every lunch time, but it's also more cost effective. You've been doing this for some time now and it is just "something that you do". Now that's great, you're being awesome without even realising it, but you're missing out on realising that every time you prep your food the night before, you're adding another small victory to the tally.

These wins and small victories can be more powerful than you can imagine. Once you begin to celebrate them, you begin to constantly reaffirm to yourself that you are actually winning and moving forward. It becomes a snowball effect, the more small victories, the more unstoppable you become.

Take a moment to think about 3 of your own small victories. These wins don't have to be recent, but shine some light on them and be proud of what you have achieved.

CHAPTER EIGHTEEN

FIX THE CAUSE NOT THE PROBLEM

All problems big and small have a cause. There is a reason why such a problem has occurred, and as a general rule of thumb, if you fix the cause, you're more than likely going to fix the problem as a by-product.

If you, or you know anybody that has ever suffered with a knee injury (not including anybody that has been struck in the knee from football, rugby martial arts etc), then it's more than likely that the knee isn't the route of the problem. Even though the knee is where the pain is and is the area that is subsequently taking the beating, we need to look at what's causing it.

The vast majority of knee pain is a result of either a lack of strength, stability or mobility around either the hip joint (above the knee) or the ankle joint (below the knee). If we team up with a specialist, they will be able to identify which area needs specific work. Once the prescribed work has been completed over a series of weeks, the knee pain should go away. You have fixed the problem not by massaging or wrapping the knee, but by fixing the cause itself.

Picture this, you come home from work one day and you notice water dripping from the ceiling. One of the pipes under the bath has come lose and has started to leak. To address the problem, all you really need to do is wipe the ceiling with a towel and "viola", dry ceiling, no more water. But an hour later you look up and the water is dripping again. To fix the cause, you head upstairs, look under the bath and tighten up the loose fitting. The water has now stopped leaking. The water may have stopped leaking, but now your spouse is giving you grief because when you were banging around in the bathroom, you woke up your new-born baby.

Most new parents go through a stage of being short and snappy with each other. They tend to squabble over trivial things that just never seemed to matter that much before they had a baby. So, although the problem itself is something unimportant, to fix it we need to look at the cause. It's not that overnight Mum and Dad have become combative with each other, it's actually because they are sleep deprived and haven't had any time together since becoming parents. My wife and I were really lucky because when our son was born, we knew this. We were fortunate enough to have grandparents who love looking after our son, and as a result we can spend time relaxing and decompressing with each other.

When a problem occurs, acknowledge it, and then go all Sherlock Holmes on the issue.

CHAPTER NINETEEN

IMPOSTER SYNDROME

Imposter syndrome can be described as a psychological pattern in which somebody doubts their skills, talents, or accomplishments and has a continuous internalised fear of being exposed as a fraud. The crazy part is that the vast majority of people who push themselves to reach lofty goals suffer with the effects of feeling like an imposter, like they have no right to do what they're doing.

This thought process can creep in, in a number of different ways in various situations. It's often found when somebody is competing at their first sporting competition. Regardless of the size and scale of the competition, a lot of newer competitors often doubt their abilities on the day. They begin to question if they're even good enough to compete, even though they have trained for this for the last 12 months, sometimes even longer. Imposter syndrome is particularly rife amongst top level CEOs and management of large-scale companies. Almost every time somebody gets a promotion or climbs another rung on the ladder, they are plunged into a role where they actually do know what they're doing, but because they have never been at this level before, they feel like they don't belong there. The further out of your comfort zone you go and the more you challenge yourself, the more likely it will be that you will come face to face with these thought patterns.

A client of mine and her daughter are in the planning phase of opening up a franchise of a well-known shop within the next 12 months. Neither my client or her daughter have done anything like this before and every time I ask her how it is all going, she talks about how she feels like she is going into it blind and with minimal experience. However, regardless of this she is super excited and is driving the process forward. They're prepared to tackle any obstacles head on, learn on the way, and open up their franchise.

So, what do you do when these thoughts occur? Acknowledge them and plough on regardless. Don't let self-doubt stop you from putting one foot in front of the other. It doesn't have to be a race, as long as you keep moving forward, you'll get to where you need to be. If you've made it this far, why can't you carry on going.

CHAPTER TWENTY

PATIENCE MY FRIEND

To acquire a skill or get better at something, it takes thousands or hours and repetitions, but what it also takes, is patience. When you first begin a new hobby or sport, you start from ground zero. In the first few weeks and months you can progress relatively quickly. Most new skills begin with learning the basics and the fundamentals, and although these are not to be overlooked and cannot be mastered straight away, they are however accessible straight away.

A prime example of this is when a beginner takes up a martial art. One of the first movements that is learnt in kickboxing is the jab. As far as techniques go this is a relatively straightforward one. In layman's terms you throw a punch with your leading hand in a straight line towards the target. The great thing about this is that everybody on their first session can throw a jab. Yes, it might not be technically great, but they can do it nonetheless. If on the other hand, they were asked to throw a jumping spinning reverse turning kick, it simply wouldn't happen.

As a beginner you pick up these basics quickly and see progress early on, but the reality is that the better you become at something and the longer you have been doing it, the harder and harder it is to move the needle. Progress slows to a point whereby on anything other than a biannual scale, you wouldn't even see it. The story goes that when Bugatti were designing the Veyron, getting the car from 0-250 mph was challenging, but getting it from 250-253 was on another scale all together.

So how do we combat this demoralising realisation? We learn to love what we do, the process, and to be patient. We must trust that what we're doing is working, even though we no longer see daily improvements. If you have had an injury, it doesn't simply go after day 1 of rehab. It can take months and then all of a sudden, "wow my shoulder doesn't actually hurt". Nobody is fluent in Mandarin after 1 lesson but in time and with patience you can be.

Learn to be patient, the progress will come, and it'll be worth the wait. Instant coffee tastes like a cup of canal water, but a real, slowly made coffee is the elixir of life. Patience my friends.

CHAPTER TWENTY-ONE

FAIL TO PREPARE, PREPARE TO FAIL

Back when I was in school, I remember my French teacher preaching to the class about how preparation was key, the week before our exam. "Fail to prepare, prepare to fail" was the phrase that she said to us all. In all honesty, I'm quite shocked that I can actually remember this. That phrase and the French words for glue stick and ruler are about all I took from year 8 French. It was only many years later that I began to see the real-life applications of the lesson that my teacher was trying to get across to a room of uninterested 12 year olds. If you don't fully prepare for something big, then you better be prepared for something to go badly wrong.

A couple of years ago, a group of 9 of us from the gym decided that we wanted to take on a challenge called "The 3 Peaks". The goal of The 3 Peaks is to summit the highest mountains in Scotland, England & Wales all within a 24 hour period. The 3 mountains consisted of Scotland's Ben Nevis, Scafell which is located in England's Lake District, and finally Snowdon in Wales. Now for anybody who is used to hiking up mountains and maintains a generally decent level of fitness, this is a very achievable task. However, because of this, this is also one of the reasons why this story has made it into this particular chapter.

The plan was to leave the gym on the Friday morning and reach Scotland in around 5 hours. We'd arrive at Fort William, go for a wander, have some food and get an early night. We were then to wake up early doors on the Saturday and scale Ben Nevis first. After making it down from Scotland's highest point, we were to jump in the cars and head south to Scafell. Here we would climb Scafell in the dark and get back down in the middle of the night. Finally, we planned to head further south to our final peak. We were to scale Snowdon and make it back down as the sun was coming up. 3 Peaks, in 24 hours, easy work.

We set off Friday morning in two cars, packed with the 9 of us and all of our supplies. We headed North up the M6 past The Lake District, all the way to Fort William where we would be staying the night. After several stops, and a slightly late departure, we arrived at our overnight destination early evening. We checked into our dorms, dumped our kit, and headed out for food.

One of the guys had booked a restaurant so that we could load up with a big meal before the main event the following morning. The idea was to spend a couple of hours there, and then head back and get our heads down for a good night sleep. However, on leaving the restaurant to walk home, one of the group spotted a pub across the road and said, "Let's go in there for one". I'd like to say that as a group we stood strong, gave a collective "No!" and walked home... but that is not what happened. At 1:30am we still hadn't made it to bed. Aside from dropping into the splits on the dance floor with Gaz, I can't remember a great deal from that particular night, but what I can tell you is that at 8am the next morning, it definitely wasn't worth it.

Now "rough" is a great way to describe how you feel after a night out, however, we were not rough, we were rotten. I attempted to open my eyes and lift my banging head off the pillow. Eyes half shut, and with yesterday's contact lenses still in place, I looked around at the sea of carnage from last night. This was not the day to climb 3 mountains.

After eventually getting ready and forcing down some breakfast, we made our way to the bottom of Ben Nevis. We loaded up, took our mandatory group picture, and started our ascent, more than 3 hours behind schedule. Even though the 24-hour window only begins as you start your climb, this delay would have a knock-on effect and mess with our timings throughout the challenge.

The initial climb went really well. The fresh Scottish air helped clear our hangovers, and once our legs had warmed up, we were on a roll. The weather bounced around between warm and cool, but at this point it remained dry. We were moving well as a group and were now closing in on the summit of mountain number 1. As we climbed into the clouds the weather began to turn. The rain began to fall, and the sun disappeared. It didn't matter though, we had now reached the summit, and it was time to hit the descent. Unfortunately, rather than leaving the rain and wind at the top where it belongs, it followed us down the mountain. This didn't just slow our pace, but it dramatically reduced our visibility too.

The problem that we were now having to deal with was that we were all completely soaked. Any waterproofs had now failed thanks to the sheer volume of rain, and my nonwaterproof t-shirt and bodywarmer that I had ingeniously decided to wear, now carried about half my body weight in water. During the descent itself, even though we were wet, we kept warm because we were constantly on the move. It was more of an irritation at this point than an actual issue.

We made it to the bottom off the mountain in one piece, but Ben Nevis had taken us 2 hours longer than planned which meant that our now tight 24 hour window had become even tighter, and the things had only just begun. The next rookie mistake that we made when we landed back at the cars, was the absence of anywhere to get changed into our dry clothes. The sky was still leaking, and the relentless downpour showed no signs of stopping. We didn't think that on a May weekend the rain would be an issue, but this is Britain, and we should have known better.

After a delayed change over, we all clambered in to our now damp and muggy cars and headed south to mountain number 2, Scafell. It was now beginning to go dark, so we tried our best to get our heads down for some rest before we arrived in the Lake District. For some extremely annoying reason, that didn't happen. I tried to shut my eyes to rest but nothing happened. Instead, I sat there surrounded by my damp clothes and was thankful for my short femurs whilst stuck in the boot of an SUV. Several hours later and in the pitch black, we pulled up at the foot of Scafell.

Even though we were all in a bit of a state, spirits at this point were quite high. The car journey had given us just enough rest to get some charge in our batteries so that we could tackle our next peak. We emptied out of the cars, donned our jackets and rucksacks, and got ready to set off. To start up Scafell we had to cross a small field before hitting the rough stuff. The ground was muddy as hell but fortunately the sky was clear. I remember looking up at the stars and thinking how epic the view from the top of the mountain is going to be under the moon on a night like this. With headtorches fired up, we began to make our way up our second peak.

During the ascent of Ben Nevis, we made it to the summit before any issues reared their ugly heads, but this time, it was a different story. On the way down peak number 1, my knees began to ache thanks to the repetitive pounding and constant readjustments that had to be made because of the slippery terrain. It also didn't help that I didn't have walking boots, I was wearing CrossFit trainers. I must admit I even baffle myself sometimes with my bright ideas. Once we had reached the cars and they had had chance to rest, the aching had subsided by the time we reached Scafell. However, after only 30 minutes of hiking, my left knee began to scream.

I knew at this point we had at least another 2 hours of climbing before we reached the summit, and I tried to forget about the fact that once we reach it, we then have to come back down. Refusing to show weakness or to let the team down, I sucked it up and hobbled on. As we progressed up the mountain, the weather began to get worse. What was at first light drizzle, rapidly became horizontal rain. Our limited visibility had practically disappeared and to make matters worse, we were now lost.

Unfortunately, there is no well-lit path up the mountain, and because it was now the middle of the night, we had already past the only other hikers that were daft enough to attempt this in such weather. With nobody to offer any assistance it was now all on us. Fortunately, Gaz had an extremely basic GPS device that pretty much saved our bacon. He was able to navigate us through a boulder field and back towards some kind of clearing.

Cold, wet, tired, at this point all we wanted to do was get the fuck off that mountain. After clearing the boulder field, we finally debated the option of turning back. Not only were we all shot, but the reality had set in that this was no longer safe. The group was full of injuries, we had no phone signal, and people were really beginning to suffer. Lu reached a point where she was unable to stop shivering and was showing early signs of hyperthermia.

As we were about to call it, Gaz appeared from out of the gloom and shouted, "The summit's here!!". Somehow, and I still don't know to this day, we had actually reached the top of Scafell! It may have taken us an hour longer, but we had got to the top. But that small moment of joy was quickly replaced with the realisation that we now had to get back down.... and things were about to get worse.

On the way up, you move your body in a particular way. Because you're moving up hill, you lean slightly forward, and your foot hits the ground in a controlled manner with very minimal impact. My sore knee had been bothering me all the way up, but I was still able to climb with it. However, when you’re on the way down, you move in a totally different fashion. Every step down sends impact through your legs as you catch your bodyweight and stop yourself from tumbling forward.

So, it's 4am in the morning, and here are the cards that I'm holding. With the rain not letting up, I'm soaked head to toe and freezing cold. It's pitch black and I have about 3m of visibility in front of me. There is absolutely no alternative to getting down this mountain right now, there is no phone a friend or getting a piggyback. And as I take my first step down, I realise that my knees can't take it. "Fuck!".

Mercifully, I was able to stand side on, and practically crab walk without being in agonising pain. But this was slow, very very slow. It would have probably been faster bum shuffling down. To make matters worse, my wife and I began to get left behind by the group. This wasn't in a malicious way, but subconsciously because the group was so beat up and cold, they were trying to get down as fast as possible. The problem was that they were taking the GPS and all of the remaining torch light with them. I remember feeling frustrated as hell, not at the group, but at myself and the fact that it was still God damn raining in the middle of May.

Fortunately, the group decided that because I was lagging behind, that I was to go at the front and set the pace. As we slowly snaked down the mountain, Gaz shouted to me "Are you OK Josh?". Now I consider myself extremely disciplined, relatively resilient, and above all very positive. But this had broken me. "No, this is fucking shit!" I replied. It was so so slow. I felt like the equivalent of Andy Dufresne digging that tunnel with his tiny rock hammer in The Shawshank Redemption.

Finally, several hours later as the sun was beginning to rise, we made it back to the cars at the base of Scafell. Our bodies were in tatters, our morale was somewhere in Fort William, and nobody had any dry clothes left to change into. It was now apparent that without a helicopter, there was no way of us completing peak 3 in under the 24 hour mark. Nevertheless, we slowly climbed into the cars and headed south towards Snowdon.

After a short time on the motorway, we pulled into the services. Gaz who was sat in front passenger seat turned around and looked at Rach, Ste and me. He jumped out and headed over to the rest of the group in the second car. After a couple of minutes, he reappeared. "Right, they're all dead. You're not going to make it up Snowdon are you?" he said to me. "I'm not going to lie, I really don't want to, but if the rest of the group is going for it, I'll crawl up it", I replied in a deflated tone. "Right, we're calling it". As much as I don't like to give up on something that I've started, I have never been so relieved as I was at that moment.

With the decision made, we called it and headed back home. As much as "The 2 Peaks 1 Piss Up" is something that we all laugh about now, there was a lot to be learnt from our experience. We had not prepared, and as a result we had failed. Hindsight is a wonderful thing and looking back there are countless things that we could and should have done. For a start, we should have not got leathered the night before, I think that's a given. Some of us, mainly myself were extremely under equipped in terms of clothing and gear. I had done no previous hiking either, so even though I consider myself fit, my biscuit knees simply weren't conditioned to scaling mountains.

We had underestimated the scale of the challenge and paid the price. So as my French teacher said many years back, "Fail to prepare, prepare to fail."

CHAPTER TWENTY-TWO

BE TOUGH AS HELL, BUT KNOW WHEN TO ASK FOR HELP

If something is worth doing, you're going have to be tough to get through it. Whether it be physically or mentally, the more challenging the task the greater degree of toughness required. That being said, there comes a point that even the most resilient of people need to seek out help, and that is not a bad thing.

If you're going to be competitive at sport, you're going to get injured in one way or another. Some people have great careers and only have to deal with minor niggles, pulls and knocks. Others have to put up with annual visits to the operating theatre to be put back to together, but that is the nature of competing and is a fact that most athletes come to terms with early on in their careers. For them, the juice is worth the squeeze.

Is there a difference though between being tough and being stupid? Yes. An important skill that a competitor can develop is the ability to know the difference between a minor ache or pain, and an actual injury. As a general rule of thumb, if one of my clients or lifters pick up a knock, let's say their elbow is twinging or their shoulder is a bit sore after their last training session, the first thing we will do is keep an eye on it. If after 4 weeks the pain hasn't subsided, it's time to seek out expert advice from a physio.

More often than not, most knocks will sort themselves out through adequate movement, rest and recovery work, without having to resort to the physio. But what we don't want to do is blatantly ignore an injury, attempt to train through it, and then make the injury significantly worse. An irritable Lat or Hip can be trained on, but a freshly ruptured ACL, maybe not. "Suck it up buttercup" is a particular favourite phrase of mine but I'm very aware of when I'm using it.

The ability to identify when you need to seek out help is an incredibly important life skill to have. We've all been through mental ups and downs, and that is part of life, but if we can ask for help or seek the advice of a family member or a close friend, we can prevent any underlying mental build ups from reaching breaking point. If you hate your job, rather than sucking it up and being miserable, maybe it's time to seek help and change your career path. Be tough and resilient, but always seek out help when it's needed.

CHAPTER TWENTY-THREE

IF IT CAN BE LEARNT IT CAN BE LEARNT

What is the most impressive feat that you've ever seen somebody achieve? Could it be a routine on the gymnastics rings that you have watched somebody perform at the Olympics? Maybe it was when Eddie Hall Deadlifted 500kg? Or what about a very skilled translator that can speak more than 10 different languages? Regardless of what it might be, all of these incredible skills have one thing in common, they were all learnt.

When somebody new starts something like CrossFit, depending on their previous training background, there are plenty of new skills that need to be learnt. From simple movements such as Kettlebell Swings and Wallballs, all the way up to Handstand Walking and Snatching. Now for the vast majority of people with no prior training experience, the idea of actually walking on their hands seems to be out of this world. Yet despite this, I have seen countless people who have hardly ever been upside down before learning how to perform this skill.

A feat that always sticks with me is the first time I heard that certain people can memorise a shuffled deck of cards, and then recall them in the same order, in under 5 minutes. Let's face it, most of us struggle to remember where we've left our car keys, or what we walked upstairs for. After stumbling across Joshua Foer's "Moonwalking with Einstein" (which I highly recommend reading), I thought that maybe this is a skill that I could actually learn.

I read the book cover to cover, and whilst I was away for the week in Cornwall, I practiced the techniques and lessons that the author talked about. The first thing I had to do was to create something called a memory palace. This is essentially a place that you know inside out. A good example could be the house that you grew up in, or maybe your place of work. I chose to use my grandma's house, mainly because she has lived there for what seems like 300 years and I have been visiting regularly since I was born. I could navigate my way through that house blindfolded, and that's pretty much the point.

Next, before you get onto the good stuff like cards, you need to start small with something like a 10 item shopping list. With this list of items, you then picture each individual item in your memory palace. Let's say the first 3 items are a wooden spoon, a bunch of grapes and some batteries. You would then in as much detail and as animated as possible, picture these items in your memory palace. For example, visualise the wooden spoon throwing a bunch of grapes to a big glowing battery with googly eyes and hands. The idea is that you're more likely to remember visuals than words. Once you have mastered small lists, you move onto larger ones, all the way up to 50 plus items. Then it's time to move onto cards. Before you can start however, you need to assign a celebrity to each card. Hearts could be sports people, clubs could be singers and so on. Now you have 52 cards, with 52 celebs. It's time to shuffle the deck and begin to pull cards out and place them along a route within your memory palace.

Utilising these tools and visualising scenarios that included Mat Fraser arm wrestling with the Easter bunny in the kitchen, whilst lady gaga was playing beer pong with Queen Victoria, to my disbelief by the time that I got home from my time away, I was able to recall a full 52 card random deck of cards in just under 8 minutes. What I thought was borderline impossible, no longer was.

If you're ever inspired by what somebody is doing, believe that you too can learn the skills to achieve what they can. Now I'm not saying that at 40 years of age you can go from never training, to reaching the Olympic stage, but if you want to become stronger, lose weight, or perhaps become more knowledgeable, whatever it may be, remember that if it can be learnt by somebody else, you can learn it too.

CHAPTER TWENTY-FOUR

BE DISCIPLINED ENOUGH TO NOT NEED MOTIVATION

Motivation can be a fickle thing. It comes and goes as it feels, you can rarely control it, and it is certainly not to be trusted. You can be sat on your couch watching the Olympics, and all of a sudden you feel motivated to start training on Monday. Then Monday comes and said motivation is nowhere to be seen. But what about Discipline?

In a game of top trumps, discipline beats motivation every time. Discipline's number one champion factor is its controllability. You can control how disciplined you are as an individual. If you're disciplined, you're disciplined, you see the job through until the end.

Your alarm goes off on a Monday morning at 5am. It's cold and dark and you sure as hell don't want to get out of your warm cosy bed. But last week you booked onto a 6am session at the gym, and now you're faced with a difficult choice. Do you get out of bed, get ready and get to the gym? Or do you allow yourself to kill the alarm and roll over? The correct answer is you drag yourself out of bed and get to the gym. Not because it's going to set you up well for the day, not because it has endless physical and psychological benefits, but because you made a promise to yourself, a promise that you would go to the gym. You are a person of your word and it's time to walk the walk.

Discipline is addictive. Once you can prove to yourself that you can do something as simple as turn up to a session at the gym, imagine what else you could achieve when you believe that you're disciplined enough to see anything through to the end.

During May of 2018, my wife and I travelled out to Italy for her cousins wedding. We stayed in a picturesque place called Umbria, which is located about half way down the country. We stayed with a group 8 in an old-fashioned rural villa, which if you're into that kind of thing is really nice. However, it was situated high up in the hills, looked down over the village, and had a pool… so it was a pretty nice place.

On the third morning of our stay, I made my way to the bathroom that connected to our bedroom and turned on the shower. After letting the water run for 30 seconds to allow it to heat up, I threw my towel over the rail and jumped in.

"AGHH SHIT!!" I yelped as I leaped back out of the shower. The lovely villa from 200 AD had ran out of hot water. The cold water had hit my skin and instantly turned me into a panicking lunatic. After calming down I stood there looking at the shower faced with a decision. I can either get a grip, muscle up buttercup and have a wash in the cold shower, or I can be a wimp and smell all day. I weighed up my options, then turned off the shower and opted for excessive anti-perspirant for the day.

For the remainder of the day I mulled over the morning's events in my head. Rather than just forgetting about something as trivial as not getting into an ice-cold shower, which let's face is it, is the normal thing to do, I couldn't help but entertain this inner urge that I had to conquer this fear. I'd heard of people taking cold showers on a daily basis, but thinking quite frankly that they were bonkers. One of my old clients used to cold shower every day without fail, and at first I thought he was crackers as well. Yes there are some amazing health benefits including a turbo charged immune system, a greater resistance to the cold and even a potential increase in natural testosterone levels, but is the juice really worth the squeeze?

Once we had returned home from Italy, I order 2 books about Cold Training, and trawled the internet for everything I could find. After doing my due diligence and research, I came up with a plan of attack. In typical performance coaching style, I wrote myself a programme based on progressive overload (that's how you get better at everything right?). The idea was that on day 1, after my normal shower, I would drop the temperature by 25 percent, and attempt to stay under the water for 5 breathes. Day 4 I'd increase the breathes to 10, and as the days went by I'd gradually build up to 20 breathes. Once I had mastered this, I would repeat the same process but with the water getting progressively colder. The one promise that I made to myself was that no matter what, I was to do this every single day. No excuses.

It's said that a habit can take anywhere between 18 to 254 days to form, depending on the person and who you ask. Numbers such as 66 days and 21-90 days are also of popular opinion. But regardless of how many days it actually takes, it always starts with day one. If you can be disciplined enough to do something every day, it doesn't matter how many days it takes to become a habit, your disciplined enough to do it anyway. At the time of writing this chapter, it has been 1176 days since I began cold showering, and I haven't skipped a single day. Hot summer days, ice-cold January mornings, it makes no difference, it has to be done.

Since starting over 3 years ago I have noticed a significant increase in my resistance to the cold and I very rarely suffer with illness. I can't comment on my natural testosterone levels because I haven't measured them either before or after, but I am certainly stronger and perform to a higher level than I did pre Cold-Training.

If you want to conquer a fear, seek out the wisdom, be consistent and get after it. If you aspire to climb Everest, go and get it. Put in the training and preparation and get yourself up that mountain. Discipline is your weapon for mass achievement.

CHAPTER TWENTY-FIVE

HOW DO YOU EAT AN ELEPHANT?

How do you eat an elephant? One bite at a time. The biggest challenges can be broken into the smallest steps. If you have ever been presented with a task that overwhelms you because of its sheer size, you've probably looked at it and thought how on earth am I going to get through this.

Last year, my coach Adam Travis decided that he was going to raise some money for a young boy so that his family could afford a new wheelchair for him. The way that he decided to raise said money was by walking 5 marathons in 5 days, a total of 131 miles. Not only is this an Everest of a task, Trav is a born and bred Weightlifter and is not built for walking long distances.

After getting through day one, his feet were destroyed. He sent me a picture of the blisters from the day's walking and to say his feet had fallen to bits would be an understatement. I remember thinking "how on earth is he going to get up and walk on those in the morning". Yet the next morning, he got up, strapped on his shoes and cracked on with marathon number 2.

On day number 3, I rang Trav just after lunch to see how he was holding up. He was in high spirits because of the cause and the reason he was doing such a crazy challenge, but he was hurting. Joints had now started to ache, and blisters were multiplying faster than rabbits. You could tell in his voice that even though he was in pain, it wasn't going to stop him. It's times like that when you realise just how slow walking is as a form of locomotion. It takes so long to cover any ground, especially when compared to running.

Regardless of the hurdles and challenges that he faced along the way, on the evening of day 5 Trav hobbled across the finish line. After over half a million steps, he had completed the 5 marathons and raised well over the target for the young boy and his family. How did he do this? One step at a time.

We can learn from this and apply it to pretty much any challenge that we want to overcome. If you have a massive pile of work to get through, maybe you're a teacher with 300 papers to mark, how do you get through it? One paper at a time. If you have dreams of making it to the Olympics, how do you get there? Internationals, Nationals, Regionals, Training Sessions, Sets, Reps. Make the bites as small as you need to, every rep you do gets you one step closer.

Whatever your task maybe, break it down into tiny chunks. Make a start and get that elephant eaten!

CHAPTER TWENTY-SIX

PAVLOV'S ATHLETE

During the late 1800s, Russian physiologist Ivan Pavlov made a very interesting discovery. Whenever he fed his dogs, naturally they began to salivate when the food was put in front of them. But what Pavlov realised was that not only did this happen upon the arrival of the food, but they also actually began to salivate when they heard the footsteps in the corridor of the person bringing them their food. The dogs had started to associate the sound of footsteps with being fed. As human beings, we can also take advantage of this realisation.

During most CrossFit metcons, you're going to have to stop to come up for air. Now that might be for 30 seconds if you're brand new to it, or even just for 5 seconds whilst breaking up a big set of wallballs. There are exceptions to the rule but for the vast majority, if you're coaching a CrossFit class you're going to see a lot of people resting. A particular favourite thing of mine to help people out is to initiate a countdown for them. If somebody is taking a little bit longer than they really need before jumping back up to the rig, it will be "Ok Rach let's get back to it, 3, 2, 1".

Now if you're in the middle of a workout, your heart rate is 150 plus and your lungs are burning, you're subconsciously going to try and seek out some comfort in the form of rest. But the thing to remember here is that you can always go just before you think you're ready, especially if it is something that isn't very heavy or highly skilled. Initiating the countdown means that rather than taking 15 seconds rest, you only take 10. If you do that every round of a 10 round workout, that's 50 seconds faster in total.

If you can implement this countdown for yourself, you can condition yourself to suck it up and crack on with the task at hand as soon as you hit "1". If you wake up in the morning and can't get out of bed, start a 5 second countdown and on number 1 get yourself out of bed. If you're doing a bungee jump and you're scared shitless, start the countdown. Walking out onto a stage, entering an interview room, whatever it is that you're about to do that either frightens you or makes you uncomfortable, the same theory can be applied.

CHAPTER TWENTY-SEVEN

THE INVISIBLE KEYSTONE

If your goal is to go to the gym and either add muscle mass or reduce your bodyfat, you can physically see the difference once it begins to take effect. You can see it with your eyes, your muscles look bigger or your waistline looks slimmer.

If you want to get stronger, once again you can see the adaptations happening. It may not be quite as obvious as your body gaining or losing size, but you can certainly see it using metrics. When you can lift a weight that you have never been able to lift before, or when you do a pull up where previously you couldn't. The same can be applied to the desire to get fitter and faster. When you hit an all-time personal best in a cycling or running time trial, it's there in black and white that you have completed the work in less time than it had taken you previously. Once again, you can see it.

But what about your mental state? What about your mindset towards trying to achieve your goal? The physical adaptation that we are working towards is very easy to quantify, but our mindset towards it is the complete opposite. Not only is it very hard to see and measure, it's also the single most important part of anything that you do.
Just as the keystone of an archway is responsible for holding up the entire structure, if your mindset isn't in the right place, everything else is going to crumble around it. The mind controls the body.

You can be at the end of a training phase where you're due to hit an all-time personal best, but on the day you're distracted by external factors, your "head isn't in it" and you flop. The body is completely ready and raring to go physically, but the mind is elsewhere. When you see top athletes messing up things on the big stage that they can normally do with their eyes closed in training, it's generally not the body that fails, it's the mind that falls victim to the pressures of competition.

Of an evening when it's time to chill out on the couch, it's very rare that you are so drained from the day that you are physically unable to move. There will certainly be a lot of mental fatigue, but if required you can still get up off the couch. So, if you have a daily stretching routine that you do every night, but you decide to skip it because you're too tired, it's not that you physically can't stretch, it's your mind that is saying that you don't want to. The hurdle is mental, not physical.

Dial in your mindset, and everything else will follow.

CHAPTER TWENTY-EIGHT

OBSTACLE OR OPPORTUNITY

Having been involved in some form of sport or training most of my life, picking up the odd injury here and there is just something that you get used to, but when the big ones happen, not only do they hurt physically, but they test your mental resilience as well.

Several years ago, I developed an irritable pain around the base of my lower back. It wouldn't hurt all the time, just every now and then whilst training it would kick off. As you can probably imagine, I simply ignored. Rather than seeking out professional advice from a specialist, I just ploughed through the pain and carried on training (what can I say, we all have to learn the hard way don't we).

This is all very well until the day that you are demonstrating a twisting lunge, and the next thing you realise you're in a heap on the floor unable to move. As I'd twisted over my front leg, I had basically added the straw that broke the camel's back... literally. I fell to my hands and knees in front of a 6am class with 10 people watching me, confused as to what I was doing. In my attempt to hide what had actually happened, I managed to sit back onto my knees, and then asked the class to start their warmup.

As soon as they had begun, I struggled to my feet using a PVC pipe and headed to the toilet, again trying to mask the pain that I was in. Why I felt the need to not let the gym know what had happened I don't know. Maybe it was a mixture of embarrassment and panic, or that I didn't want them seeing a coach broken. As I left the gym floor, I shouted over to one of the other coaches who fortunately was on the class and asked them to guide the members through the work out until I got back.

Once I reached the toilet, I locked the door behind me, and pretty much fell bum first onto the toilet. "Fuck!" I muttered to myself. Not only did I not know what was happening, I was sat fully clothed on a toilet, and was completely unable to get up. My phone was in reception, and all that I had with me was my saviour of a PVC pipe.

After several minutes, I calmed myself down and began to think straight. Squatting up off the toilet was definitely out as I physically could not get into the position do it. Fortunately, I was able to slither off the toilet and onto the floor, which is not a cool place to be in a guys' toilets. From here I was able to move onto my front, and then using the PVC pipe I was able to get back on to my feet. I had managed what my 21 year old self most Sunday mornings at 4am had not, I had escaped the toilet.

Later that morning I contacted my physio to let her know what had happened. After explaining the mornings events we scheduled an appointment for the following day so that we could start to get to the bottom of the issue. After a thorough assessment and some movement testing, we concluded that an MRI was the safest option so we could be 100% sure of what had actually occurred.

Fortunately, I was able to get an appointment for an MRI scan within a matter of weeks. During this time the pain had started to ease slightly. I was able to move around but loading in most movements was a struggle, I certainly wasn't training. So, after having the scan, falling asleep in the MRI pod, and impatiently waiting for the postman every day, the results finally came through.

As I opened the letter, I felt strangely excited, purely because once I knew what the issue actually was, I could start on my road to recovery. I sifted through all of the medical jargon and the procedural writing until I got to the actual results. The scan had revealed that I had split one of the vertebrae at the base of my back, genius over here had essentially fractured his spine. My excitement quickly shifted to concern as I realised that this wasn't simply another muscle tear, this was my spine.

On the whole, rehabbing an injury is relatively straightforward. Now I'm not saying that the job of the specialist is straightforward, because it definitely isn't. What I'm referring to here specifically is the process that an injured person follows, that is relatively simple, do your rehab work. However, from a psychological perspective it's not so easy. Not only have you got to deal with the injury, but you also have to deal with the fact that you can no longer train in your favourite sport until you are healed.

For me, a fractured spine ruled out most exercise. But could this obstacle be turned into an opportunity? Aside from me being an idiot, the root cause of my injury was down to my deep abdominal muscle being relatively weak and somewhat inactive. A combination of that and a tight upper back had become the weak link in the chain that had eventually broken. Even though I was unable to do a lot of exercises, what I could do was build a bulletproof midline and a super mobile thoracic.

The funny thing was that once I was able to return to normal training, after a few weeks I was able to hit personal bests on most of my lifts, thanks to my rehab work.

Hidden opportunities are always there, you just have to be willing to find them. If you ring up your favourite restaurant to book a table, and they have nothing available, think of this as a great opportunity for you to try somewhere new. You never know, this could become your new favourite restaurant. Next time you're stuck in a queue or in traffic, rather than getting angry at the world for dealing you Snailboy at the till, or 90 year old Brenda doing 20 mph in a 40 zone, take a moment to breathe and have some mindful time to yourself.

CHAPTER TWENTY-NINE

THE GROUP EFFECT

There is a particular phenomenon that occurs when people train, work, or compete in teams or groups. Rather than relying on just your own internal will power and drive, you actually feed off your team mates to push you further than you would alone, and to achieve results of incredible calibre.

There was a particular weightlifting session a few months back that sticks in my head. It was a Saturday morning, and everybody on the class was snatching. After a thorough warm up and some light technique work, everybody began to build up towards their percentages and working weights for the day. Everybody was moving well, they looked sharp and precise with each rep on the build-up, all the way up 90%, which was their target for the session.

The first person stepped up to their bar, began to lift, and then missed. The second person then began their lift, miss. Now when somebody reaches their working weight, everyone on the class lifts one at a time. Not only does this allow the coach to focus solely on that particular lifter, it allows the rest of the class to observe and watch. This can work really well for inspiration if the person who is lifting hits a really nice lift, but if this lifter misses, it can go the opposite way. After the second miss, the entire class then proceeded to miss each of their lifts one after another. This was no coincidence. How can everybody go from hitting 85% beautifully, to all missing 90% without a single hit.

After the first wave of misses, I headed over to each lifter individually to reassure them and level their heads. Here's the crazy part. The first person on the class to miss 90%, then stepped up to the bar and hit their lift, comfortably! The second person immediately followed with the same outcome. Surprise surprise the entire class then continued to hit their next lifts. Now don't get me wrong I do consider myself a good coach, but I'm not a barbell witchdoctor. All it had taken was for one person to make a good lift to subconsciously inspire the entire class to hit theirs.

As a human being you are massively influenced consciously and subconsciously by the people surrounding you. If you're grinding through a god-awful task, whether that is a project at work, an endurance event, or an absolute slog of a rugby game, if you're whole team is suffering with you, it makes that suffering that little bit more manageable. Not only does it feel like you're sharing the load, but you also have the ability to feed off each other's strength and drive. If you're climbing a mountain in a group of 10 and you start to dip, there are 9 other people around you that can help pick you up. This can be incredibly powerful.

When the whole team is down, it only takes one person to start the ball rolling. One person to head to the front to punch a hole in the struggle so the team can draught. One becomes two, two becomes four, and the next minute the whole team is firing on all cylinders again. Matt Fitzgerald talks about this in great detail is his brilliant book" How bad do you want it".

CHAPTER THIRTY

FEEL THE LIFT

When coaching Weightlifting this is something that we talk about a lot. These movements are so complex and happen so fast, that you don't have time to be overthinking what is going on. If you do attempt to analyse a lift as you're doing it, you're going to find yourself missing more lifts than you hit.

Rather than thinking about every single aspect of the movement, pick one thing in particular and just feel what is going on. If you're going for a big Snatch, you could focus on "staying balanced", or "stand all the way up".

Picture a footballer taking a penalty. During training, he places the ball in the corner of the net and beats the keeper 9 times out of 10. Nice and controlled, nice and relaxed. He is simply thinking about where he wants the ball to go, and then he sends it there. What he's not doing is thinking about the movement from start to finish. Every step on the run up to the ball, how he needs to balance on his none kicking leg, how much force he needs to put though the quad and hip flexor to strike the ball, and so on. Imagine the outcome if that was the thought process? This is also a contributing factor on game day. If the pressure is on for a match winning penalty, the great players can block out everything external and simply take the kick as if they were on the training ground. A less experienced player would be susceptible to the effects of the big stage. They'll over think, overcompensate, and are more likely to miss.

If you have ever had to perform a speech at wedding, you'll know that when you're rehearsing it on your drive to work every morning, you absolutely nail it. You're articulate, witty, and your jokes are hilarious. Once you learn your script, you're in a flow state of presentational excellence. Then the big day comes, and you begin to overthink everything. What if nobody laughs, what if I stumble or forget my lines, but the truth is that if you simply relax, focus on just speaking as you have practiced, you will absolutely nail it. Always shine light on the things that can go right, as opposed to the things that can go wrong. If you visualise yourself performing a great speech or hitting a beautiful lift, it is much more likely to happen than if you focus on potentially missing or fumbling your words.

CHAPTER THIRTY-ONE

I FEAR THE MAN WHO HAS PRACTICED 1 KICK 10,000 TIMES

"I fear not the man who has practiced 10,000 kicks once, but I fear the man who has practiced one kick 10,000 times." The point that Bruce Lee was making with his famous quote was that if you practice one thing relentlessly, you can become exceptionally good at it. However, if you spread yourself too thin, you simply become either average, or really bad at a lot of things.

Now from a sport point of view, I want to discuss 3 separate training disciplines: CrossFit, Weightlifting and Running. For anybody that has never heard of CrossFit, CrossFit athletes are some of the fittest on the planet. Their sport requires them to be able to weightlift, perform high skill gymnastics, run, swim and be able to complete gruelling metabolic conditioning workouts. The cream of the crop, the CrossFit Games athletes, can do all of the above to an extremely high standard.

That being said, let's bring in Weightlifting. Weightlifters specialise in 2 specific competition lifts, the Snatch and the Clean & Jerk. These lifts are also performed by CrossFitters, but they are just 2 of a myriad of skills that they have to master. As a result of a Weightlifters specificity, they are on the whole, better at Weightlifting than CrossFitters. If you take Guilherme Malheiros, the 90kg CrossFit Games athlete Snatched 138kg at the 2021 Games Max Snatch event. Now this is an impressive lift, however if you compare it to 81kg Lu Xian Jun's 170kg Snatch at the 2020 Tokyo Olympics, that really puts things into perspective. Now there are some outliers, Tia Toomey who is arguably the greatest CrossFitter of all time has also competed in Weightlifting at the Olympics, which is incredible.

Now let's bring running into the equation. The top male from the 2020 Olympics completed the marathon in just under 2 hours 10 mins, and the top female in just under 2 hours and 30. Are the CrossFit Games athletes going to be able to do this? Not likely. What about the Weightlifters? I think we all know the answer to that one.

The reason Weightlifters, Runners, and any other single discipline athletes are so good at what they do, is because that is all they do. That is their kick that they have practiced 10,000 times.

As a Weightlifting and CrossFit coach, I am often asked how to get better at Snatching. The simple answer is spending more time on Snatching. It may mean that other things have to take a bit of a back seat, but if you want to become significantly better at a difficult skill, it needs to be your focus.

If you decide you want to learn another language, let's take Spanish for example, you should spend time practicing and learning Spanish. You also want to learn Wing Chun, take up cooking lessons, join a chess club, work a 40-hour week, learn to play the Cello and learn how to break dance. By all means give this a go, there is nothing wrong with having a variety of hobbies, but if you want to be really good at something, you need to pick one and focus on it.

It's the equivalent of having only one piece of butter. You can spread it over one piece of toast, and it will be epic, or you can try and spread it over 8 pieces and have 8 rounds of dry Sahara Desert tasting bread.

CHAPTER THIRTY-TWO

THE BAD DAY SPECTRUM

You finish your gym session, and you deem it as a "bad session". You were meant to be hitting 5 sets of 1 Back Squats at 90% of your max, but on one of the reps your technique was off, and you failed the lift. Even though you hit the other 4, this one stays with you and haunts you for the rest of the session.

Now if we think of this as a bad session, this has the potential to turn into a bad week. A bad week into a bad training cycle, a bad cycle into a bad year. Next thing you know you're convinced that you suck, and you throw in the towel. However, if we shift our thought process, the bad session can be considered the other way round. The bad session wasn't bad at all, just that particular exercise didn't go well. Let's go even further, it wasn't even the exercise, it was just 1 bad rep.

Here's another example. Your alarm goes off at 6am and interrupts you when you were quite clearly halfway through your sleep cycle. You grab your phone to turn off the alarm and see what time it is. Not only have you accidentally set your alarm an hour late, but your phone slips out of your hand and smashes you in the face.

You dive in the shower, have a quick wash, get out, and then you notice that your wife had put all the towels in the wash the night before. So, after drying yourself with a couple of dry face flannels, you brush your teeth, throw your clothes on and run downstairs. You go to the cupboard and grab the egg box and the bacon from the fridge. The bacon is out of date and there is only one egg left. I think we can all agree, this is a "bad morning".

As you head out for work, one of two things can happen, the morning's events can set the tone for the day and allow you to focus on every little thing that could potentially not go your way, or you can see it for what it actually is. Is this bad morning going to become a bad day, a bad week, a bad year? Or do you laugh it off and think next time I set my alarm I'm going to double check.

A friend of mine once told me he was having a bad year because his holiday had been rearranged, and his car had been scratched in a car park. I think it's fair to say that if those two things were the only two negatives in the last 12 months, you'd say that's actually not a bad year at all.

Don't let a bad rep become a bad session, don't let a bad morning become a bad day. Acknowledge it, accept it, and move on.

CHAPTER THIRTY-THREE

STRIKE WHILST THE IRON IS HOT

I'm a huge fan of sticking to your programme and not trying to kill yourself every session, but I am also a massive advocate for striking whilst the iron is hot.

Most training cycles will be aiming towards some form of peak. That could potentially be a competition or an event, or simply just to hit some new all-time best efforts. For arguments sake, let's say you're following a 12 week programme. You head into the gym on week 5 and you start warming up. You feel epic. You've had a great night's sleep, you have eaten well the day before and your pre-workout has just kicked in. Your percentages are feeling lighter than they have ever felt before, but your programme for today says that you're only to work to 80% of your max.

Now you have two choices. Number 1, you stick to the percentages and move on. Another session in the bag, pennies in the jar and you're one step closer to test week (the final week of the 12 week cycle). Or number 2, you go for gold whilst you're feeling great. Now unless you're meant to be deloading or you have a competition imminent, my answer would always be if you're feeling good, go baby go! The vast majority of my all-time personal best lifts have actually happened midway through most of my cycles, and the same can be said for many of the lifters that I coach.

Now in an ideal world, when test week arrives you will go into it in an optimal state. Well rested, well fed, low stress, no injuries and so on... but we're human and that is not how life works. Imagine training on a 12 week cycle, you stick to your percentages every session, even when you're feeling great you don't go higher, and then when test week finally comes round disaster strikes. The Sunday before test week, you have an argument with your partner, you realise that financially you're struggling, and your neighbours have decided to throw a house party that night.

You wake up Monday morning feeling like you've been hit by a train, mentally, physically and emotionally. You get to the gym that evening and surprise surprise, you under perform. This mental defeat now sets the tone for the week, and you fail at absolutely everything. The following week another 12 week cycle begins and before you know it, it's been over half a year and you still haven't maxed out effectively.

The idea of striking whilst the iron is hot can be applied outside of training as well. Although in a slightly different manner, the principle is the same. You bump into a friend in the supermarket, and you agree to meet up for a coffee and a proper catch up. "Let me know when you're free", "I will do". The conversation goes something like that, and you both part ways and you never go for that coffee.
You're brushing your teeth of an evening and you think to yourself that it's been over 12 months since you last went to the dentist. You decide that you should really go and book in for an appointment, but once you finish brushing your teeth, you put your toothbrush back and go to bed. Another 12 months pass, you're missing a tooth and you still haven't been to the dentist.

Next time you want to make plans with a friend, book it in your diary there and then whilst it's fresh in your mind. Next time you need to go to the dentist, book it in there and then. Now don't get me wrong these thoughts don't always appear at the most convenient of times, so where possible write them on your notes or to do list for later. Strike whilst the iron is hot!

CHAPTER THIRTY-FOUR

TRUST YOUR COACH

If you're trying to be successful at something, it's pretty much guaranteed that if you seek out a coach, mentor or expert in that particular field, you're more likely to succeed.

Your coach is your guide to help show you the way from where you are, to where you want to be. The great thing about having a coach is that they have already walked the path that you are on. They have learned from experience both the dos and do nots of their area of expertise. As a result, under their guidance you can achieve your goals much more efficiently than if you were to try and figure it all out on your own.

Something I always like to highlight when talking about having a coach, is that not only do they tell you what you need to be focusing on, but also what you don't need to worry about. If you are beginning a career in Weightlifting, something that newer lifters don't realise is that even though in competition, everybody does the same 2 main lifts (Snatch and Clean & Jerk), there are countless different styles and techniques for these movements. The Chinese have a certain way of Cleaning, that may differ from the Russians, that may differ again from the Bulgarians, and again for the Americans. Now thanks to the glorious internet, most of this information is readily available to confuse the life out of a beginner.

The best bit, some styles can have the absolute opposite of views on certain aspects of the lifts, meaning that if you simply try to take bits unknowingly from different styles, you end up with a car crash of a lift, or even worse a severe injury.

It's not just in Weightlifting either. If you want to learn how to play the guitar, you seek out somebody who is great at playing the guitar and who is an equally great teacher. If you're looking to develop and grow your business, you find a highly successful business coach to guide you through the jungle. But regardless of the area that you are being coached in, above all you must trust your coach.

If you don't trust in the person who is teaching you, then you may as well part ways there and then. You can be given the most powerful piece of advice available, but if it comes from a source that you don't trust, you're going to ignore it. Are you going to take financial advice from a poor person? Or maybe piano lessons off somebody that can't play the piano?

Of course not, it's like getting flying tips from a penguin, you don't trust them because they're not a valid source.

If you have the right coach, believe in what they are teaching you, and above all, trust them.

If you're looking for a coach, would like to learn more about Weightlifting, or you would like to learn how to become fitter, stronger and live for longer, check out my website www.joshsummersgill.co.uk and get in touch, I would love to hear from you.

CHAPTER THIRTY-FIVE

BE INSPIRED NOT DISHEARTENED

Nowadays thanks to tools like social media, it's very easy to feel like everybody is better than you and that they're achieving everything that you aspire to do. You can see people with huge houses, the car you've always dreamed of and holidays in places that you can't afford. If you train, you'll see people in your sport outperforming you in every metric. Runners and rowers hitting much faster times than yours, weightlifters and powerlifters moving weights that you can barely roll, and bodybuilders' and crossfitters' abs bursting through more abs. All this can do a great job of making you feel insignificant, but only if you allow it to.

What if we change our thought process? Rather than be disheartened by what we see, we can be inspired? At present, I currently compete in weightlifting. My goal is to compete at the highest level that I can reach and see how far I can push myself. Weightlifting is great example to demonstrate this point because it's a numbers game. For me to win gold at the world championships, I would have to add more than 100kg to my lifting total. To put that into perspective, I'd have to increase my total by 40%. Granted this is a monumental task but seeing the cream of the crop lifting these numbers simply shows me that it is actually possible to do so. Nobody thought it was possible to run a 4 minute mile until Roger Banister, and then look what happened.

If you want to be successful, whether in business, sport or any other area of your life, look at the people that have already made it in that particular field. Who are they, what do they do and how do they do it? Learn from them and allow their achievements to inspire you.

CHAPTER THIRTY-SIX

SACRIFICES MUST BE MADE

The greater the level that you wish to reach, the greater the level of sacrifice that will have to be made. To become truly great at something, you have to dedicate countless hours to mastering your craft. These countless hours aren't free, you only have so many hours in any given day, and they have to be moved from one pot into another pot. The more time you spend on honing your skills, the less time you will have for other aspects of your day.

To achieve what we can refer to as an adequate baseline of strength and fitness for "General Physical Preparedness", you can do so by only giving up an hour of your time a day 3-5 days per week. However, if you want to compete as a body builder, and walk around at single digit body fat percentages, it's going to take a lot more than that.

As well as the hour you have already dedicated, you will have to add on an extra hour a day for the added training volume. Then you can also add a further 2 hours a day for your nutrition, including food shopping for 300 chicken breasts, cooking and meal prepping, and eating every 2 hours 8 times a day. These also aren't exciting great tasting meals, you're not going to be able to enjoy all of those rich flavoursome foods that we all love. Bland will become your new best friend, along with egg whites, broccoli and rice. Don't forget, if you have to go out for a family meal to a restaurant, you'll have to bring your meal prep with you and pass on the cheesecake.

If you want to become a champion weightlifter, you're going to have to sacrifice pleasant training. You're not going to be able to get away with only squatting once a week, you'll have to do it almost daily. You're going to pick up niggles and injuries along the way as you push your body to its limits. You're also going to have to pass on the weekly Saturday nights out on the raz.

Here' the scenario. You go out drinking all night, and you stumble through the door at 3am. You pass out and don't move until lunch time the following day. You spend all Sunday in a lethargic hungover mess because the 9 hours of sleep that you had during your coma, wasn't actually sleep. You were simply unconscious and wasted a full night of precious sleep. Not only that, but Sunday is also normally your rest day where your body recovers from the battering it has received through last week's training. Instead of recovering and growing from training, it's busy dealing with the aftermath of being poisoned by 8 Jagerbombs and 6 Sambucas. You wake up Monday, attempt to train, and you can't even hit your percentages. You've now wasted a training day and taken a step backwards.

You have to ask yourself is the juice worth the squeeze? Do you want to get to the top more than you want to get plastered every Saturday? For most people the answer is no, and that's why only very few people make it to the top of their sport.

When my wife was studying for her degree to become a nurse, she had to make sacrifices. As well as grafting away at a challenging degree, she was also working full time to still cover her bills. She had to say no to socialising with friends and going out doing the things that she enjoys whilst she concentrated on her course work and studying. My wife is now an incredible A&E nurse, not only does she love her job, but she also spends her time in work saving people's lives. Sacrifices were made, but the juice was definitely worth the squeeze.

Before heading into the next chapter, take a moment to think about what you want to achieve. Whether it is training related, maybe it's to do with your career or business, or it might be something different altogether, but think about what you truly need to do to get there. What do you need to do, and what do you need to sacrifice to reach your goal?

CHAPTER THIRTY-SEVEN

MOVE WELL, THEN HEAVY

As the old saying goes, "Don't run before you can walk". Don't try to do a back flip if you can't jump properly, and don't try and squat 200kg if you can't squat properly with your own bodyweight. If you focus on moving well before moving heavy, you will eventually be able to move heavier for much longer.

A good way to think of this is by imagining a set of tyres on a car. Under normal circumstances the tyres wear down at a normal rate. As long as you're not rallying about like a mad man, smashing into potholes, and your tracking is aligned, you will get the full life span out of the tyres. Your joints are your tyres.

To help ensure a long training life and the ability to prevent injury as best we can, we need to first look at movement quality itself. Let's take the Front Squat as an example. Picture this, you see somebody at the gym load up a barbell, unrack it, and begin to Front Squat. As they begin to squat you notice that their rack position where they hold the bar is questionable. They are only able to hold the bar with a single finger on each hand, and their elbows are pointing towards the ground. An optimal front squat rack should have the elbows forward and up, and most of the fingers around the barbell.

As they descend into the bottom of their squat, you also notice that their ankles begin to collapse inwards, and then their knees begin to follow. The final thing that you see is that as they drive up out of their squat, their back begins to round and the whole lift begins to shift forward. You let out a sigh of relief as they survive the rep, until to your horror you discover that it was only rep one of five! It doesn't take a biomechanics specialist to spot bad movement. You could show this squat and that of an elite weightlifter to a 5 year old and they would be able to tell you which one is more optimal.

If you want to do something to your greatest ability, it's important to spend time to master the basics. Don't let excitement and giddiness misguide you into progressing onto things that you are not yet ready for. Take your time, master the basics.

CHAPTER THIRTY-EIGHT

LEARN TO SAY NO

Often times when we're asked to do something, depending on who is asking we can feel obliged to say "Yes". Even when the actual answer that we want to give is "No", we still agree because it's easier to do so. If somebody is asking you do to something, it is a request of your time, and you are not obligated to say "Yes". Obviously, there are exceptions, if you're in work and your boss asks you to do your job, if your mum tells you to tidy your bedroom, or if your spouse asks you to do the dishes that you have left out from your breakfast, in these situations it is within our best interests to say "Yes".

The same applies from a training perspective. If you're following a particular programme, you need to stick to it. Even if your friends are pestering you to do a workout with them or something that isn't in your session, if you don't learn to say “No”, you will end up burning out and getting nowhere. If one of your friends or family members asks you to do something that you really don't want to do, say “No”. Now there are means and ways of doing this. Don't just abruptly say no, suggest an alternative or give a genuine reason as to why you don't want to do that particular thing with them. Again, if you don't like somebody, I personally wouldn't be as blunt as to say “I'm not doing that because I think you're an A Hole”, there are ways of politely declining.

The other problem that arises with always saying yes, is that you can only agree to so much. You agree that you're going to go somewhere with a friend, but then on the day of the event you let them down because you never actually wanted to go there in the first place. You then become somebody who lets people down, a bailer, an unreliable person. If you say you're going to do something, follow through with it, but you can only do so if you learn to value your own time and say “No”.

CHAPTER THIRTY-NINE

EAT THAT FROG

There's an age old saying that basically states that if first thing in the morning, you wake up and eat a frog, then in theory this is the worst thing that you'll have to do all day. As a result, you'll have got the least desirable task done before anything else so that you don't have to do it later.

We all have stuff to do that we put off. It can either get put off until the end of the day, end of the week, or even indefinitely. In the same way that back in the days of getting swole in the Globo gyms, you'd put off leg day until there was no other equipment free... and even then, you'd just go in the pool instead. When really what we should have done is hit legs on a Monday, and then crush arms and chest for the remainder of the week.

I was talking to a friend of mine whilst training not so long ago. He was coming towards the end of his session, but he still had some accessory work to do. We had a conversation about how much he hated doing this glute and ab work, and how he dreads it every session. Even though he didn't enjoy it as much as snatching or squatting, he still cracked on and got the work done because he knew how important it was. Quite a high percentage of people have underactive glutes, even those who train, and this can lead more often than not to knee pain. Combine that with lots of Weightlifting and CrossFit and your knees are going to feel like broken digestives. If you fire up your glutes now, hopefully you won't have to rehab your knees later.

If you've got a list of jobs to get through at home or at work, if you attack the worst one first, then that son of a bitch won't be hanging over your head all day. There is also less chance of it getting pushed back to the never never. Author Brian Tracy talks in detail about this concept in his book "Eat That Frog", which I would definitely recommend reading if you haven't already.

CHAPTER FORTY

THE RIGHT TOOL FOR THE RIGHT JOB

Have you ever tried to pick a lock with a golf club? Neither have I but I can imagine it would be impossible. Whatever you're setting out to achieve, it's important that you have the correct tools for the job. If you're trying to get stronger, you should be following a strength programme, if you're trying to get better at running, you should be following a running programme etc. Your body is incredible at adapting to the stimulus provided, so always remember that the stimulus you give it, needs to line up with what you're trying to achieve.

One of the girls that I work with decided 12 months ago she wanted to complete an Ironman. She had previously run, cycled and swam before but nothing as extreme as a full distance Ironman. As a result of her change in goals, her training obviously had to change to suit. Over the 12 months that followed, she became fitter and fitter, her body became leaner, and she had effectively programmed her body into endurance mode.

After completing the iron man and having a great event all round, we checked in several weeks later to discuss the event itself and our plans going forward. Something that was highlighted to me was that a couple of weeks after the race, she had attempted some strength and conditioning work that she used to do prior to her Ironman training, and she was shocked at the results.

Her leg strength in her words "had totally disappeared". She recalled the bar and the weights feeling incredibly heavy in comparison to 12 months earlier. This may seem strange at first but if we look at what her body had been primed for over the last 12 months, it was not absolute strength. An ironman does not require somebody to have a tremendous 1 rep max back squat, what it does require however is a set of legs that are resilient enough to be able to work for a 12 hour plus race. A combination of training and a drop in bodyweight contributed to her back squat dropping, but also allowing her to successfully complete her goal and finish her Ironman.

If you want to go for a 4 week driving holiday, you're not going to choose a formula 1 car, in the same way that you're not going to be racing in a Ford Galaxy. If you want to scale a mountain, you wear hiking boots, not CrossFit trainers (I know right, lesson learnt). Remember that whatever it is that you're setting out to achieve, make sure you have the right tools for the job.

CHAPTER FORTY-ONE

HOW YOU DO ANYTHING IS HOW YOU DO EVERYTHING

Your time is your finite currency, you only have so much of it and once it's gone it's gone. So, if you're going to invest some of your precious time into doing something, you might as well do it right!

If you're going to take time out of your day to go and train, then it's going to have a greater positive effect if you make the most out of the training that you do. If for example your programme starts with 3 sets of 5 bench press, rather than just banging out reps to tick a box and get it done, make the most of every set. How much growth and potential can you squeeze out of every single rep. Unless you're doing a CrossFit metcon whereby the objective is to complete the workload as fast as possible, perform each rep for quality. If you're just mindlessly hitting your 3x5, you're missing out on potential adaptation. This is the equivalent of winning £100 on the fruit machine and just leaving £50 where the money comes out.

If you're a competitive athlete, not doing something properly can have heart breaking results. Let's say you're a weightlifter, and every time you finish your jerk, rather than standing momentarily with the bar fully extended overhead, you drop it before showing control, this will then become your movement pattern or "muscle memory". If you do the same thing every time you jerk, this will become second nature and you won't even realise you're doing it.

There was an incident at the 2020 Tokyo Olympics which highlights this perfectly. One of the male lifters hit his clean & jerk, and instead of holding the bar overhead and waiting for the down single from the referees, he dropped it early. The lifter celebrated because he thought he had got the lift, but because he didn't wait for the down signal, it was deemed as a "no lift". Now there are other factors in play, but what you practice becomes permanent, and this poor athlete paid the price.

If you can learn the trait of doing something properly, it can carry over into almost anything that you choose to turn your hand to. Even the trivial tasks of day-to-day life. Recently I've been in the process of baby proofing our living room for our 8 month old menace. After sticking rubber corner protectors on, I realised that I'd missed off one of the sticky pads. My first thought was "It'll be fine", and then my second thought was "He's going to pull this off and either eat it or give to the dog". So practicing what I preach I took off the protector and did the job properly.

If it's worth doing, it's worth doing well.

CHAPTER FORTY-TWO

PERCEPTION IS REALITY

If you perceive something in a certain way, that becomes your reality. If you perceive something as good, then to you it is good, and likewise if you perceive something is bad, then to you it is bad.

If we talk about something being "heavy", it is totally relative. We could say that 20kg isn't heavy for a Deadlift, but I think we'd all agree that it is heavy for a pencil. The actual weight itself hasn't changed, 20kg is still 20kg. For the next example, let's theoretically place a barbell into the rack and load it up to 40kg. I am now going to ask you to unrack the bar and Strict Press it overhead. Let's say that your best ever Strict Press is 45kg, so it is fair to say we're pretty close to max effort.

If I were to ask you just before you press, "Does that feel heavy on your shoulders?", the likelihood is that you'll say

"Yes", and rightly so, a near maximal lift will feel heavy. However, if once you have completed your Strict Press, I then ask you to Front Squat the same barbell (current best ever of 100kg), we're probably going to see something different. If you were presented once again with the question of "Does that feel heavy on your shoulders?", the answer is more than likely going to be no, due to 40kg being less than half of your best front squat. So, is this bar heavy or not? Getting psyched out of a lift simply by the bar "feeling heavy" is one of the most common ways for a lifter, particularly a newer lifter to miss or bottle a lift.

The same can be said for a set of dumbbells. Most people would struggle to curl 20kg dumbbells but would be able to Deadlift them. The weight itself has still not changed, only the task at hand, which can influence your perception.

Is rain a bad thing? It's cold, it's wet, and it can ruin any outdoor plans that you may have for that particular day. In Britain we love to moan about the rain, which is strange really because it rains here for around 11 months a year. But is it a bad thing? Our frequent rain helps create the amazing greenery and lakes, and it ensures that the likelihood of a draught is dramatically reduced.

Rain itself isn't a bad thing, it only becomes a negative if we perceive it in such a way.

Be conscious of your perception.

CHAPTER FORTY-THREE

USE IT OR LOSE IT

Our bodies are remarkable. They are incredibly capable of adapting to whatever stimulus we place upon them. If we want to get fitter, we subject them to conditioning. If we want to get stronger, we apply strength training protocols. If we want to become more intelligent, we read and learn. Now without question this process is truly amazing, however there is a flip side to it. Yes, your body will respond to a stimulus, but it won't distinguish between one which is positive and one that is negative.

At the time of writing this book, we have all had to deal with a particularly strange time. Thanks to COVID-19, the vast majority of the population have had to take time away from their work, hobbies and sports. This unprecedented period of time away from our normal activities has applied a different stimulus to our bodies. As a result of being away from what we do for so long, our bodies have become deconditioned, and adapted to not having to carry out the demands of our day-to-day lifestyle.

If you are a weightlifter or crossfitter, your hands will more than likely have been ripped to bits during your first week back to training. The same can be said for anybody who plays a racket sport, or anyone who performs a manual hands-on job. The calluses that had built up on your hands have long since gone and your palms have turned into tissue paper. Your hands will have adapted to not having to deal with being battered on a daily basis.

After your first week back at training, your poor body will be broken. Just like that horrible first session after a 2 week holiday, only this time exponentially worse. After an 18 month period your body will have adapted to a more sedentary lifestyle. If your body doesn't need something, like precious muscle mass that you've built up from the gym, the chances are that it's going to get rid of it. That muscle mass was only there as a result of an adaptation. If it's not going to be used it's not going to be kept. It really is a case of use it or lose it.

Now don't get me wrong, if you've trained for years at something, you're not just going to lose it overnight. But it's important to know that if you want to keep something a certain way, you need to work at it. Constantly feed your body with the correct stimulus so that you can achieve the results that you want.

CHAPTER FORTY-FOUR

SHARPEN THE SAW

If you have ever had the pleasure of using a blunt saw to cut through a piece of wood, you know how tedious of a task it can be. You feel like you're sawing away for hours and getting nowhere. You have two choices, carry on working away at your current pace, or stop what you're doing to go and sharpen your saw. The question you have to ask yourself, "Is it worth taking the time out to go and sharpen your blade? Will this save you time in the long run?".

Let's say you have a goal to back squat 100kg. Your current max is 70kg, and your training is going well. Your squat has been increasing steadily and you know that eventually you will hit the 100kg mark. However, when you squat, your ankles roll inwards, and as a result you can't utilise an optimal drive through your legs. Now the blunt saw will eventually cut through the piece of wood, but it would be far more efficient to take the time to sharpen it. If you were to take the time to fix your ankle issue, whether that is mobility, stability or a combination of the two, you are not only going to reach the 100kg more efficiently, but that 100kg back squat is going to be executed with great form. And as we know, great form equals longevity.

When I left secondary school at 16, I went to work with my stepdad installing bathrooms. One of the big parts of the job was tiling. Now being somewhat arty, I enjoyed tiling because it's something that if you have done a good job, it's very noticeable.

There was a particular job on a particularly wet and rainy day where I was cutting a tile to go around the door frame. The cut itself was relatively complex and was the type of cut that is normally done on something called a wet cutter. The wet cutter however was sat outside in the pouring rain, ironically getting wet. Rather than sucking it up and going outside, I decided to try and cut the tile using a set of grips. I sat there and nibbled off part of the tile bit by bit, until 15 minutes later, I had almost finished. With only a tiny bit of tile left to go, I gripped the tile too hard, and it shattered. Not only did I have to start again, but I was now 20 minutes behind, and I still ended up getting wet. Lesson learnt, do it now to save time later.

CHAPTER FORTY-FIVE

YOU DON'T NEED THE PERFECT HAND

When you're playing a game of poker, if you pick your cards up after the deal and you see that you have been dealt a pair of aces, the likelihood that you're going to play that hand is pretty high. Two aces is one of the best hands that you can be dealt so naturally you're going to be instilled with confidence and are going to carry on. However, these hands don't come around that often, and if you were to only play when the perfect hand gets dealt, you're going to get wiped out by the blinds and the more skilful players. A pair of aces is great, but you can also still win with a 7 and 2.

If you look at elite performance in sport, the athletes at the top are a combination of several aspects, one of which is genetics. Now, genetics are what you're born with, if you're born tall or short, you're not going to change this. The vast majority of top-level basketball players are well over 6ft, and the vast majority of jockeys are well under 6ft. This is because to get to the highest level, your body needs to be optimal for that specific sport. I could have the best training in the world, but I'm never going to be able to dunk a basketball like Jordan because I'm 5ft 6. Just like my friend Craig isn't going to win the grand national because he's 6ft 3 and weighs 100kg.

So, does all this mean that if you don't have the perfect genetic make up for what you want to do that you should simply not do it? Absolutely not! Yes, it does make a difference at the top but that shouldn't be a reason to stop you from doing something that you enjoy.

Over the past few years, I realised that something I am really passionate about is writing. The interesting thing is that I'm slightly dyslexic, I completely miss words out when I'm writing without even realising it. It's only when reading it back weeks later that I can see that it doesn't make any sense. Back in high school I took Art as one of my options, despite the fact that I was colour-blind, and managed to pass with an A star. If it was a case of only playing with the pair of aces, I wouldn't have chosen Art and I would never have written this book.

Now I'm not saying don't play to your strengths, but if you really want to do something then don't make excuses either. If you want to start training or join a gym, don't "wait until you're a bit fitter", or "when your ankle is a bit better", make a start with what you want to do and enjoy it regardless.

CHAPTER FORTY-SIX

RIDE THE WAVES

When training, you have good sessions and bad sessions. In life, you have good days and bad days. The important thing is not to lose your mind on the bad days, but to be prepared for them when they arrive. There is no escaping bad sessions and bad days, but what we can learn to do is capitalise on and appreciate the good ones, and accept the bad ones. It's just a case of powering through until the storm passes.

On the good days and good sessions, you can ask more of yourself. You can push that little bit further, work that little bit harder and you can feel like you've made a month's worth of progress in a day. On the bad days, ask a little less of yourself. Ease off the accelerator and just hit the minimum effective dose. If it's a bad session, do what you can, even if it's lighter or slower than normal, but tick the box regardless. If it's a bad day, free up your schedule and try to fit in some 'you time'. If it can wait until tomorrow, then it can wait. You are your biggest asset, and you need to be kind to yourself.

I remember having a conversation with my dad back when I used to work in the office. At the time I was in the process of transitioning between my current job to full time gym owner, but financially it was a minefield. As a result, on this particular day the mental clouds had well and truly rolled in and I was feeling pretty deflated. I explained to my dad how I was feeling about the whole situation and why I was feeling so low.

He then began to explain to me how Winston Churchill used to have bad days, and on these days, he would refer to a black dog. On these black dog days, he'd feel like a black dog was following him around like a dark cloud of misery. As a result, he would become extremely unproductive and unmotivated on that particular day. But the important part is that when these days were coming, they could be identified and dealt with accordingly.

The punch that you expect hurts less than the one that you don't see coming. Every single person on the planet has good days and bad days, we all have to ride the waves and experience the ups and downs. As long as we can learn to realise this, we can then learn to deal with the bad days and bad sessions when they show up.

CHAPTER FORTY-SEVEN

ONES & ZEROS

When it comes to completing something that you have set out to do, you are going to come up against resistance. This may be from close friends, your peers or even your adversaries, but regardless of this you simply plough through like you can't even hear their criticism. If you want to do something whether against the grain or not, finish the job regardless of judgement.

My Friend Phill and I often joke about a story he tells of when he was younger and training in a commercial gym. He hadn't been training long so as with most of us at first, his knowledge of training was limited to "Bi's and Tri's". He recalls seeing a guy lay on the floor in the top of a press up position, doing what Phill thought were just extremely poor depth press ups. "What an idiot, what are those?" were the thoughts of judgement. It's only years later that we now know that this guy wasn't doing the world's worst press ups, he was performing an exercise called a scap press up. A particular exercise that is performed for scapula stability and shoulder health. 10 points to Gryffindor.

If you're brave enough to step out of your comfort zone and go for something epic, then you owe it to yourself to ignore the judgement of others. Keep it simple, it's black or white, a one or a zero, you either do it or you don't. If you want to open up a business doing something absolutely mental, then do your due diligence and go for it. If you want to go to the Olympics, work your arse off and go for it.

The bottom line is that we are all in control of our own lives. We steer the ship, and what others think of your choices is their problem and not yours.

CHAPTER FORTY-EIGHT

YOUR SHOELACES AREN'T A PRIORITY IN A WARZONE

Many years back, I went through this phase of going over the top with trying to be healthier. My heart was in the right place but looking back now, it was never going to be sustainable. I'd make a point of trying to only drink out of glass bottles in case plastic contaminated the water that I drank. I bought only organic fruit and veg, and avoided food groups that I had read were "bad".

At the time, I was training regularly with one of my good friends Stu. We went for a coffee one day after training and rather than my normal cappuccino, I ordered a black coffee. After querying my unusual choice of coffee, I explained to Stu that I had decided to stop having milk in my coffee because of some arbitrary reason that quite frankly, I can't remember. Stu laughed and replied "but don't you still have cereal for breakfast? That's the equivalent of being in the middle of a warzone and worrying that one of your shoelaces has come undone". And you know what, he was bang on.

It can often be quite easy to get distracted with small details or inconsequential tasks, when really what we need to be focusing on are the bigger problems at hand. If somebody is back squatting and their knees knock into each other even at a low weight, then worrying about something like grip width on the bar is irrelevant. Regardless of how wide this person has their hands on the bar, the knees are still going to knock together if that main issue is not addressed.

If somebody who has no previous training background is looking to lose weight and change their lifestyle, method dependent you're going to address calories in vs calories out before you go into details about vitamin intake and protein timing. Yes, these things are important, but only once the main elements have been taken care of.

The main trap is that the smaller secondary issues are easier to fix. It was easier for me to take milk out of my coffee (I have no issues with milk by the way, I drink it nowadays) than to change my breakfast all together, in the same way that it's easier to sit there with no calorie control and just eat chewie multivitamins.

Many smaller changes can and certainly do add up to creating a massive change, but if they are not the main problem, they shouldn't be your number one priority. Focus on the big fires first, and then put out the smaller ones.

CHAPTER FORTY-NINE

LIONS DON'T CONCERN THEMSELVES WITH THE OPINIONS OF SHEEP

If you're going to go for something in life, people are going to have something to say about it, either positive or negative. Everybody is entitled to their opinion, but you are also entitled to disregard every single one of them if you see fit to.

If you're training at the gym, and let's say for example you have started a new programme, other people in there are going to have something to say about it, unless you train in a commercial gym in which case, you'll just get judged silently by everyone with their headphones on. "Why are you following that programme? You should do this one instead", "Don't do that exercise, this one is better", "You'll damage your knees if you squat" and the list goes on.

These naysayers can think what they want, but you stay true to you. If you enjoy Powerlifting and want to progress as far as possible and see what your body can do, don't concern yourself with everyone else's judgement about what you're not doing. The likelihood is that if you're competing in Powerlifting then you're probably not going to be doing a lot of cardio, and that's absolutely fine, because it's the requirements of your specific discipline.
Now, if you are training and somebody who's opinion you value gives you some advice, then that's a different story. You know that this help comes from a place of knowledge and trust and is more likely to be worth listening to. Not just some random's personal opinion on what you're doing in the gym.

Whether you're getting a new car, going on holiday, opening a new business or starting a new hobby, these decisions of yours are going to clash with somebody's personal opinion... good. If you want something, go after it, it's nothing to do with anybody else, your goals are your goals and don't let the haters tell you otherwise.

CHAPTER FIFTY

STOP COMPETING EVERYDAY

When you compete, regardless of the sport, your body goes into a state of readiness. Not only physically, but psychologically as well. You physically push yourself past points that you wouldn't reach in training because your goal is to beat everybody else and win. You need to be better than your opponent and make sure you come out on top, which takes a massive psychological toll as well. After most competitions, competitors will take anything from a couple of days to even a couple of months to decompress and recover from the event. Without this mental and physical rest, the body would simply not recover.

So, if we were to come into the gym every day, with the sole purpose of beating the guy next to us, what is going to be the most likely outcome? Your body is going to be plunged into competition mode, every single session. Now this might be great for a week, but once you reach a certain point, your body is going to nosedive. One absolutely epic training session doesn't make you better, it's the culmination of countless consistent training sessions that truly allow you to become fitter faster and stronger. If you're competing yourself into oblivion every day, you simply won't be able to recover naturally, which will eventually lead to burn out and injury.

If a salesperson goes into work every day, and all they're bothered about is selling more cardboard boxes than their colleague Dave, is this the same scenario? We can argue that the physical demands on the body are not that of a competition, but consider this. Dave comes into work and isn't feeling great, he only sells 10 boxes that day, less than half what he usually sells. Because all you're concerned about is beating Dave, you sell 11 and then call it a day. Although you have technically sold more than Dave, you have also sold yourself short. You work on commission, and you've just missed out on another 9 or 10 boxes worth, purely because you're focusing on what Dave is doing.

The same is true during training. Training is also commission based. If you're only obsessed with beating the person next to you, then when they have a bad day you're going to coast, beat them, and pretty much waste your session and get nothing from it. Not only can competing push you over the threshold of adaptation, in this case, it can prevent you from even entering the sweet spot.

There's a good reason that a well-balanced training cycle is based on varied loads, intensities and volumes. Killing yourself everyday just isn't sustainable. Yes, you should push yourself every day, but within reason. Work in a high gear and work hard, but pressing that Nitrous button every day is going to end badly.

FINAL WORD

As a final word, I want to say thank you for taking the time to read this book. I hope these lessons help you as much as they help myself and the people that I have been fortunate enough to coach. If something in particular has resonated with you, reach out to me and let me know. If all I have managed to do is help at least one person, then writing this book will have been worth it.

Whatever you want to go after in life, go and get it. We don't get another bite at the apple, so regardless of what others say, if you want to achieve something, get after it.

Instagram: @joshsummersgill #MovingTheNeedle
Website: www.joshsummersgill.co.uk
Email: info@joshsummersgill.co.uk

REFERENCE SECTION

Snatch: A barbell movement where the bar is taken from the ground to overhead in one smooth motion. Typically, the Snatch is performed with a wide grip on the bar and is caught in the bottom of an overhead squat before being stood up to complete the lift. The Snatch is one of the 2 competition lifts performed in Olympic Lifting.

Clean: Another barbell movement where the bar is taken from the floor, but unlike the Snatch, the bar finishes on the individual's shoulders, not overhead. The bar is pulled off the ground to such a height that the individual can catch the bar in the bottom of a Front Squat, and then stand up the bar to complete the lift.

Jerk: This is a barbell movement where the bar starts on the individual's shoulders, and with the help of a powerful drive from the legs, the bar is launched overhead and secured with straight arms. There are many styles of Jerk, one of the most common is the Split Jerk. This is when the bar is caught with the legs in a split position.

Clean & Jerk: This is the second of the 2 competition lifts from Olympic Lifting. This movement is essentially a Clean, followed by a Jerk.

Back Squat: A squat variation where the barbell is positioned at the top of the individual's back.

Front Squat: A squat variation where the barbell is positioned on the individual's shoulders just in front of the neck.

Deadlift: A barbell movement where the bar is taken from the floor to the hips. The movement is finished once the individual is stood up fully with the bar, legs straight and shoulders behind the bar.

Clean Pull: This is part of the Clean. The Clean Pull is the part of the Clean when the bar is taken from the ground and is elevated by the legs. The Clean Pull finishes just before the individual relocates under the bar into a Front Squat.

Strict Press: The individual stands up with the bar on the shoulders, it is then pressed overhead without a drive from the legs.

Kettlebell Swing: The individual stands up and holds a kettlebell between their legs. From here the kettlebell is swung upwards when the hips are violently extended.

Wallball: A large medicine ball is thrown at a target on the wall, and as it descends the individual catches the ball and then rides the movement down into the bottom of a squat. The squat is then reversed and the ball is once again thrown at the target.

Metcon: Short for Metabolic Conditioning, this term is basically used to describe a high intensity CrossFit style workout.

NOTES SECTION

Printed in Great Britain
by Amazon

71849535R00118